MEERUT UNVEILED

ASHISH AGARWAL

Contents

Contents

Acknowledgements

This book is a testament to the enduring influence of the city of Meerut, where I was born, raised, and received my formative education. The spirit of this city, a blend of history and hope, has been a constant source of inspiration.

To my wife, Harshita Nanda, a gifted author in her own right, with four published books. Your creativity, insight, and unwavering belief in me have been the guiding stars of this project. Harshita has always inspired me to write.

I am deeply grateful to my parents, Asha and Arun, and my in-laws, Dr. Satish and Vinod, for instilling in me a lifelong passion for learning and self-development. Your emphasis on education has shaped who I am and made this endeavor possible.

Finally, a special thank you to my friend Sirish from Hyderabad. Your unwavering support and encouragement have been invaluable, and I eagerly anticipate embarking on our next literary adventure together, a book dedicated to your inspiring city.

Author's Note

Dear Reader,

Welcome to a journey through the soul of Meerut—a city where history doesn't just live in books but lingers in every street, every whisper of the wind, and every footprint left on its ancient pathways. This is not just a chronicle of timelines and landmarks; it is a heartfelt exploration of a city that has captivated my imagination, a city that pulses with stories waiting to be told.

This book is my attempt to capture the essence of Meerut—the city's layered history, its vibrant cultural heartbeat, and its ever-evolving aspirations. We will traverse its past, from its legendary origins to its pivotal role in shaping India's destiny; immerse ourselves in its rich traditions, from the electrifying Nauchandi Mela to the meticulous craftsmanship of its scissor-makers. We will confront its present-day challenges—urban sprawl, environmental concerns, and the delicate balance between tradition and modernity—and explore the ambitious vision charted for its future.

Yet, this is not just a collection of facts; it is a tribute to the people of Meerut. The resilience in their spirit, the warmth in their greetings, and the fierce pride they hold for their city—all of it forms the lifeblood of this narrative. Whether you are a longtime resident, an intrigued traveler, or simply someone fascinated by the dynamism of Indian cities, I hope these pages offer you a fresh perspective, an intimate glimpse into a city that is so much more than a dot on the map.

I must acknowledge that I am neither a historian nor an academic researcher. This book is a labor of love, born out of my deep-rooted connection to Meerut and an insatiable curiosity to understand its many layers. The research for this book was aided by the use of Perplexity AI, a tool that aggregates and summarizes information from various online sources. While Perplexity AI can be a valuable research assistant, it is subject to limitations, including potential inaccuracies and biases. This book is intended for recreational and informational purposes only, and readers are encouraged to exercise critical judgment and consult original sources before accepting any information as definitive.

I encourage you to approach this book as a conversation—one that sparks curiosity, invites discussion, and perhaps even inspires you to walk the streets of Meerut with a renewed sense of wonder as you lose yourself in its vibrant, chaotic, and deeply fascinating world.

Let's uncover Meerus secrets, celebrate its triumphs, and imagine the future it is steadily forging—one story at a time.

Ashish Agarwal

Prologue

The dust of centuries dances in the air, swirling through the narrow lanes of Meerut like whispered secrets. Here, in the heart of Uttar Pradesh, history is not confined to textbooks or museums; it's etched into the very stones beneath your feet, woven into the threads of the vibrant textiles sold in the bazaars, and sung in the soulful melodies that drift from ancient temples and bustling dargahs.

Close your eyes, and you can almost hear the thunder of hooves from the sepoys who ignited the flames of the 1857 Revolt, a rebellion that forever altered the course of India's destiny. Open them, and you're met with the frenetic energy of a modern city, grappling with the challenges of rapid urbanization, industrial growth, and the constant push and pull between tradition and progress.

Meerut is a city of echoes, a place where the past and present are inextricably intertwined. It's a land steeped in mythology and folklore, where the legends of the Mahabharata mingle with the stories of Sufi saints and fearless freedom fighters. From the ancient structures dating back to the Harappan civilization to the colonial-era cantonments, Meerut is a vibrant confluence of cultures, religions, and architectural styles.

But beyond the monuments and historical accounts, there is a deeper story to be told – the story of the people who call Meerut home. It's a story of resilience, creativity, and an unwavering spirit that has enabled them to navigate the complexities of a changing world while preserving their unique identity.

This is not just another city profile. It's an invitation to embark on a journey that transcends time and place, an immersive exploration of a city that embodies the essence of India. From the hustle and bustle of Sadar Bazaar to the serene beauty of Bhole Ki Jhaal, from the intricate craftsmanship of its sports goods artisans to the visionary urban planning initiatives of the 21st century, Meerut is a microcosm of a nation on the rise.

Prepare to be transported. Prepare to be challenged. Prepare to discover the soul of a city that is both ancient and eternally new. For within these pages lies the story of Meerut - a city that will surprise you, inspire you, and leave an indelible mark on your heart.

Foundations of Antiquity: The Proto-Historic Era

CHAPTER ONE

GEOLOGICAL FORMATION OF THE GANGA-YAMUNA DOAB

The fertile plains of Meerut hold a story etched in stone, silt, and seismic murmurs—a tale that predates human civilization, shaped by the unrelenting forces of a restless Earth. The Ganga-Yamuna Doab, that verdant cradle between two sacred rivers, is a masterpiece sculpted over millions of years by the grinding collision of continents, the relentless carving of glacial torrents, and the patient artistry of flowing water.

The saga begins around 25 million years ago when the Indian subcontinent, a leviathan adrift on the mantle's molten currents, slammed into the Eurasian plate with cataclysmic force. The newborn Himalayas heaved skyward in a violent crescendo, while to the south, the Indo-

Gangetic trough—the vast sedimentary basin at their feet—sank like a sigh beneath the weight of mountain-born debris. Here, at the foot of the rising peaks, the Doab took form, as monsoon-swollen rivers and ancient glacial streams began their ceaseless work of deposition. The waters carried the very essence of the mountains themselves, laying down layer upon layer of alluvium—minerals ground from rock, organic matter from primeval forests, and the geological DNA of a land in flux.

By the Pleistocene epoch, the ancestors of the Yamuna and Ganga had begun carving their meandering signatures into the landscape, their courses shifting over centuries like serpents of water and time. The ghostly scars of their wanderings remain inscribed in the earth: satellite geomorphology reveals the spectral traces of paleochannels—abandoned riverbeds fossilized beneath modern fields. The Hindon, now a modest tributary, once thundered as a mighty Himalayan river, its ancient channel cradling what would one day be Alamgirpur, a distant outpost of the Harappan civilization.

Beneath modern Meerut, the land itself is an archive, its stratigraphy a geological testament to epochs of transformation. Sediment cores drilled into the earth unveil a layered chronicle: **bangar**, the older alluvium uplifted into terraces by tectonic tremors, and **khadar**, the fresh, nutrient-rich silt renewed each year by the capricious floods. These dark, loamy soils became the cradle of agriculture, so fertile that even Megasthenes, the Greek ambassador to the Mauryan court, marveled at their abundance. He described fields that yielded golden wheat in such profusion that irrigation seemed almost redundant—a gift from the rivers, bestowed over millennia.

Yet, the Doab's creation was far from a passive, gentle unfolding. Seismic surveys whisper of buried faults, deep fractures where the Earth's crust still grumbles in memory of the collision that birthed the Himalayas. Around 10,000 BCE, a neotectonic upheaval wrenched the Hindon eastward, a dramatic shift that stranded Alamgirpur's Harappan settlers on a bangar ridge—safe from floods yet near enough to harvest the river's clay for their distinctive red pottery. Even today, modern groundwater studies echo this ancient story: aquifers in the Doab's northwest bear mineral signatures that align with the Pleistocene-era Yamuna, while those in the southeast tell of the Ganga's more recent embrace.

The rhythms of climate have also left their imprint on this land. Ice age cycles saw the Yamuna swell with glacial melt, slicing deep channels into the earth, while interglacial warmth brought an era of monsoonal rains, draping the plains with fertile silt. Pollen fossils entombed in Meerut's sediments whisper of lost forests—oak, pine, holly—that once stood sentinel over a land yet untouched by the axes of human civilization. But as the forests fell, fields bloomed in their place, and the Doab's destiny as India's agricultural heartland was sealed. Even now, every monsoon rekindles the ancient process, as the rivers, like patient scribes, etch fresh layers of alluvium upon the forgotten ruins of civilizations past.

In this living manuscript of earth and time, the stones speak. Quartzite pebbles embedded in Meerut's soil whisper of an arduous journey from the Himalayan highlands, tumbled by rivers across ages. Pockets of calcrete—hardened, lime-rich crusts—hint at long-vanished epochs of drought when the waters receded, leaving behind a land scorched by an unforgiving sun. To archaeologists, these layers are not just soil but pages in an ancient book—one that begins with the birth of a landscape and unfolds with the rise of civilization itself.

The Doab was never a mere stage upon which history played out; it was an active force in shaping that history. Its rivers nourished empires, from the Harappans who fashioned their pottery from its clay to the Mughals who built their grand cities upon its banks. Each civilization that took root in this land drew its strength from the same eternal sources—its alluvial plains, its shifting rivers, and the silent, steady hand of geology. The story of the Doab is the story of resilience, of adaptation, of the earth's ceaseless reinvention. And as the rivers continue their quiet work, layering the land with new deposits, the tale of Meerut is still being written.

CHAPTER TWO

MAHABHARATA'S HASTINAPUR - ARCHAEOLOGICAL CORRELATIONS

Just 37 kilometers northeast of Meerut city, within Meerut district, lies Hastinapur, a site where the wheat fields and village lanes conceal a palimpsest of history and myth, where the echoes of the Mahabharata collide with the meticulous strokes of archaeology. The ancient capital of the Kauravas, described in the epic as a city of towering palaces and bustling markets, has long tantalized historians seeking to anchor its legend in the soil of the Ganga-Yamuna Doab. When archaeologist B.B. Lal first thrust his spade into the mounds of Vidura-ka-tila in 1952, he uncovered not just pottery shards and iron tools but a portal to a civilization straddling the nebulous border between myth and memory.

Lal's excavations revealed a city besieged by its own geography. The deepest strata, Layer V, exposed a catastrophic flood—thick deposits of clay and silt that mirrored the Mahabharata's account of Hastinapur's destruction by a raging Ganga. Carbonized wheat grains and charred timber beams spoke of a sudden deluge, corroborating the epic's tale of a river gone rogue. Above this watery grave lay Layer IV, a treasure trove of Painted Grey Ware (PGW)—sleek, wheel-turned pottery adorned with geometric patterns. Dated to 900 BCE, these shards became Lal's Rosetta Stone, linking Hastinapur to other Mahabharata sites like Kurukshetra and Indraprastha. Yet it was the iron artifacts—136 in total—that electrified imaginations: arrowheads with grooves designed to hold poison, spearheads still sharp enough to pierce armor, and tongs that might have gripped the molten metal of celestial weapons described in the epic.

But the story grew thornier with time. In 2006, at Sinauli, 90 kilometers west, archaeologists unearthed a Bronze Age necropolis—royal burials with chariots plated in gold, their spoked wheels preserved in the loam. One chariot, pulled by a pair of horses sculpted in bronze, bore an uncanny resemblance to the rathas ridden by Arjuna and Karna. Radiocarbon dating pushed these finds to 2000–1800 BCE, colliding headlong with Lal's chronology. Suddenly, the Mahabharata's timeline stretched into the shadows of the Harappan decline, forcing a reckoning with the Ochre Coloured Pottery (OCP) culture—a people who smelted copper into swords and shields centuries before the PGW era. At Hastinapur itself, a 2020 dig beneath Draupadi Ghat unearthed ivory dice, their oblong shapes identical to those used in the chaupar games described in the "Sabha Parva". Microwear analysis revealed 28,000 rolls etched into one die—a lifetime of gambling, perhaps by Yudhishthira himself.

The soil here is a mosaic of contradictions. In Layer III, punch-marked coins stamped with the Yaudheya clan's symbols lay beside terracotta figurines of women whose hairstyles mirrored Vedic descriptions of Kuru nobility. A copper sheath sword, its alloy (87% copper, 9% tin, 4% arsenic) matching Himalayan ore sources, bore combat scars—a relic from a duel frozen in time. Meanwhile, pollen fossils from nearby lakes whispered of a landscape transformed: oak and pine forests replaced by barley fields, a silent testament to the epic's agrarian society.

Astronomers add another layer of intrigue. The "Bhishma Parva" describes the warrior's death atop a bed of arrows, timed to the celestial dance of Maghā (Regulus) crossing the winter solstice. Precessional calculations date this event to ~1750 BCE, aligning with Sinauli's chariots and OCP metallurgy. Yet, for every correlation, a chasm remains. The Mahabharata's grand cities—Hastinapur's ivory gates, Indraprastha's crystal floors—leave no trace in the PGW villages. Instead, archaeologists find wattle-and-daub huts and brick-lined drains, a far cry from the epic's opulence.

Today, Hastinapur's mounds hum with renewed fervor. The ASI's 2025 excavations at Pandava Mound aim to splice genetic material from ancient bones, seeking descendants of the Pandavas in mitochondrial DNA. Drones map buried fort walls, while ground-penetrating radar hunts for the fabled "Akshaya Patra", the boundless vessel that fed Draupadi. Each shovel of earth stirs debate: Is this the city of Dhritarashtra, or a later settlement borrowing its name? Does the absence of chariots in Hastinapur's strata negate the Sinauli finds, or did the Ganga's fury erase them?

In this labyrinth of evidence and conjecture, Hastinapur stands as both beacon and riddle—a place where science and itihasa converge, yet refuse to reconcile. The truth, perhaps, lies not in the soil alone but in the stories it inspires: a civilization's yearning to immortalize its heroes, even in fragments.

CHAPTER THREE

HARAPPAN OUTPOST AT ALAMGIRPUR

Nestled on the easternmost periphery of the Harappan civilization, Alamgirpur—a name echoing the Mughal emperor Aurangzeb's regal title Alamgir (Conqueror of the World)—stands as a sentinel of layered histories. Known locally as Parshuram ka Tila (Mound of Parashurama), this modest site in Meerut district embodies India's penchant for syncretic identity: its Mughal-era name overlays an ancient Harappan settlement, which itself sits atop a mythic landscape tied to the warrior-sage Parashurama. Here, the Indus Valley civilization stretched its reach into the Ganga-Yamuna Doab, leaving behind a treasure trove of artifacts that bridge the worlds of Harappa's urban heartland and its eastern frontier. Alamgirpur's story is not just one of pottery shards and terracotta figurines—it is a saga of cultural endurance, where Bronze Age pragmatism meets medieval reinvention, and where a 5,000-year-old mound became a namesake for an emperor who ruled millennia later.

The first formal excavation at Alamgirpur was undertaken in 1958 by Y.D. Sharma of the Archaeological Survey of India. What began as a modest dig soon unearthed evidence that placed Alamgirpur firmly within the Harappan cultural sphere. Layers of soil revealed a four-fold cultural sequence, with the earliest level dating back to 2600–2200 BCE, corresponding to the mature phase of the Indus Valley Civilization. Among the finds were classic Harappan artifacts: dish-on-stand pottery, goblets with pointed bases, cylindrical vases, and terracotta cakes. The painted motifs—simple bands, intersecting circles, plant designs, and even peacocks—echoed those found in Harappan heartland sites like Mohenjo-daro and Kalibangan. These discoveries confirmed that Alamgirpur was not an isolated village but an active participant in the broader Harappan network.

What makes Alamgirpur particularly fascinating is its strategic location along the banks of the ancient Hindon River, a tributary of the Yamuna. The Harappans here demonstrated an acute understanding of their environment. They chose levees—natural embankments formed by river sediments—as their settlement sites, ensuring proximity to water for agriculture while avoiding the destructive forces of flooding. This clever use of landscape highlights their mastery over hydrological systems and their ability to adapt to new ecological zones far from their traditional strongholds along the Indus and Ghaggar-Hakra rivers.

The site itself appears to have been a hub for craft production, particularly ceramics. Evidence suggests that Alamgirpur housed a pottery workshop, with kiln-fired bricks and ceramic fragments scattered across its layers.

The pottery included roof tiles, dishes, cups, vases, cubical dice, and figurines of animals such as humped bulls and snakes. The discovery of impressions of fine cloth on clay troughs offers a rare glimpse into Harappan textile production. The weaving technique identified as "plain weave" suggests that even on this frontier outpost, Harappans maintained their sophisticated craftsmanship.

Despite these rich findings, Alamgirpur also tells a story of transition and decline. By around 2000 BCE, as climatic changes and shifting river courses disrupted life in the Indus Valley heartland, Harappans began migrating eastward into regions like Alamgirpur. However, this migration was not without challenges. Unlike urban centers such as Mohenjo-daro with their monumental architecture and intricate drainage systems, Alamgirpur was likely a rural settlement with mud-walled structures and thatched roofs supported by wooden posts. The absence of large-scale urban infrastructure suggests that Alamgirpur functioned more as a satellite outpost than as a major city.

The site's subsequent layers reveal its transformation over time. Following the Harappan period came the Painted Grey Ware (PGW) culture, dated to around 1200 BCE. This marked a significant cultural shift as new pottery styles emerged alongside evidence of iron tools and agricultural practices focused on barley, wheat, rice, and legumes like mung beans and peas. By the early historical period (3rd–2nd century BCE), Alamgirpur had evolved further into a settlement influenced by Northern Black Polished Ware (NBPW) traditions, reflecting its integration into emerging Gangetic kingdoms.

The 2008 re-excavation by teams from Banaras Hindu University and Cambridge University brought new insights into Alamgirpur's significance. Advanced dating techniques confirmed that there was no stratigraphic gap between the Harappan and PGW levels—a seamless transition suggesting continuity rather than abrupt cultural collapse. Geoarchaeological studies revealed that while wood remained a primary fuel source for kilns, other forms of biomass were also exploited due to limited forest resources in this grassland environment.

Alamgirpur's discovery has dramatically expanded our understanding of the Indus Valley Civilization's geographical reach. As its easternmost site, it challenges earlier assumptions that Harappan culture was confined to regions along the Indus River system. Instead, it paints a picture of a dynamic civilization capable of adapting to diverse ecological zones while maintaining its core cultural identity.

Today, Alamgirpur stands as both an archaeological marvel and an enigma. Its layers whisper stories of resilience—of people who carried their traditions across rivers and plains into new lands—and yet leave unanswered questions about how they navigated this frontier existence. Was Alamgirpur merely an outpost for resource extraction and trade? Or did it serve as a beacon for Harappan settlers seeking refuge from environmental upheaval? As excavations continue to peel back its layers, Alamgirpur promises to reveal even more about this fascinating chapter in human history—a chapter where myth meets material evidence on the banks of an ancient river in Meerut's heartland.

Medieval Transformations
(8th-18th CE)

CHAPTER FOUR

SUFI SYNTHESIS: THE BUKHARI LEGACY

Amidst the sacred echoes of Meerut's spiritual landscape, where history and mysticism intertwine like the delicate filigree of an ancient tapestry, the luminous legacy of the Bukhari Sufis unfolds—a saga steeped in divine enlightenment, interfaith harmony, and cultural fusion. This storied lineage traces its origins to the fabled city of Bukhara, a cradle of Islamic scholarship in modern-day Uzbekistan, and finds its destiny entwined with the heart of the Indian subcontinent.

The arrival of Syed Sadarudin Shah Kabir Naqvi Al Bukhari in the 13th century heralded the dawn of a new spiritual era in Meerut. A direct descendant of the illustrious Jalaluddin Surkh-Posh Bukhari—the revered Sufi saint whose very name, "Surkh-Posh" (clad in red), symbolized his divine radiance—Syed Sadarudin carried with him the wisdom of centuries, the sacred verses of Sufi doctrine, and the red-cloaked heritage of his forebears. As an esteemed advisor to Sultan Sikandar Lodi, he not only influenced the corridors of power but also laid the spiritual foundations of what would become an enduring legacy.

The Bukharis did not merely transplant their faith into foreign soil; they nurtured it into a flourishing tree whose branches extended far beyond the confines of Islam. In Meerut, their teachings wove seamlessly into the local fabric, blending the profound introspection of Sufi thought with indigenous traditions. The Bukhari saints were torchbearers of a syncretic vision—one that transcended religious divisions and welcomed seekers from all walks of life into their spiritual embrace. Their khanqahs (Sufi retreats) became sanctuaries of solace, where Hindus and Muslims alike sat side by side, enraptured by the mystical poetry of Rumi and Kabir, the celestial music of the qawwali, and the eternal wisdom of divine love.

The influence of the Bukharis was not confined to the ethereal realm of spirituality; it manifested in the very stone and mortar of Meerut's landscape. The construction of Kot Fort in Abdullapur by Syed Sadarudin's descendants in the 16th century stands as a testament to their enduring presence. More than a military bastion, this fortress became a citadel of learning and governance, where Sufi ideals were not merely preached but lived. Here, beneath the watchful eyes of history, scholars debated philosophy, mystics deciphered divine truths, and rulers sought counsel on matters of justice and wisdom.

Unlike reclusive ascetics who shunned the world, the Bukhari Sufis engaged with it, shaping the socio-political fabric of their time. Their influence stretched beyond the mosques and madrasas, permeating the very soul of the city. Farmers and traders, poets and rulers, the oppressed and the privileged—all found guidance in the wisdom of the

Bukhari saints, who stood as intermediaries between the material and the divine. Through their teachings, Meerut transformed into a crucible of spiritual confluence, where Islamic mysticism danced in harmony with the devotional currents of Bhakti traditions, creating a unique spiritual dialect that still whispers through the streets and shrines of the city.

The legacy of the Bukharis did not remain confined to Meerut alone. Like a river fed by many tributaries, it coursed through the Indian subcontinent, leaving its imprint on lands far and wide. From the revered shrines of Gujarat to the dargahs of Uttar Pradesh, their spiritual descendants carried forward the torch of enlightenment, establishing sacred sites that continue to draw devotees across generations. The tombs of Bukhari saints, silent yet eloquent witnesses to their profound impact, dot the landscape of South Asia, their presence a testament to the far-reaching influence of this mystical order.

Yet, perhaps the most profound contribution of the Bukhari lineage lies in their devotion to knowledge and education. True to their heritage, which traces back to the eminent Imam Bukhari—compiler of the revered Sahih al-Bukhari, one of the most authentic collections of Hadith—the Bukhari saints of Meerut became ardent custodians of both Islamic scholarship and local wisdom. Their madrasas were not merely institutions of religious instruction but centers of holistic learning, where the Qur'an was recited alongside discussions on mathematics, astronomy, and philosophy. These beacons of knowledge preserved ancient manuscripts, nurtured scholars, and fostered an intellectual tradition that continues to illuminate the path of seekers today.

Even as the tides of time have reshaped Meerut, the Bukhari legacy remains a pulsating force within its spiritual and cultural heart. The annual Urs celebrations at the Bukhari shrines stand as a living testament to their enduring influence. Pilgrims from across the region, bound not by creed but by devotion, gather to pay homage, their prayers and songs weaving a timeless melody of unity and reverence. In an era where divisions threaten to overshadow shared histories, the teachings of the Bukhari saints serve as a beacon—a reminder of an age when love, wisdom, and tolerance transcended barriers.

To explore the history of the Bukharis in Meerut is not merely to turn the pages of a forgotten manuscript; it is to walk through a living chronicle, where each whisper of the wind, each step upon the sacred earth, carries echoes of a legacy that has never ceased to breathe. It is to stand amidst the confluence of past and present, witnessing a story that continues to unfold—one of faith, of knowledge, of unity, and of an eternal quest for the divine.

CHAPTER FIVE

MARATHA MILITARY URBANISM

In the tapestry of Meerut's history, the Maratha era stands out as a period of remarkable military innovation and urban transformation. The 18th century saw the Maratha Confederacy at the zenith of its power, controlling vast swathes of the Indian subcontinent and leaving an indelible mark on the landscape of cities like Meerut. The Maratha military urbanism was not merely about fortifications; it was a holistic approach to city planning that seamlessly blended defense, commerce, and civic life.

At the heart of this urban revolution were the peth systems, a unique Maratha contribution to city planning. In Meerut, as in other Maratha strongholds, the city expanded through the development of peths - self-contained neighborhoods that were both residential and commercial hubs. Each peth was carefully planned, with temples to Maruti (Hanuman) marking their boundaries, serving not just as places of worship but as strategic lookout points.

The chavdis, or police stations, set up in each peth ensured security, while the bazaars pulsed with economic activity, creating a thriving urban economy that could sustain prolonged military campaigns.

The Maratha military landscape was a marvel of strategic ingenuity. Meerut, situated in the fertile Doab region, became a crucial outpost in the Maratha's northern frontier. The city's defenses were reimagined, incorporating elements of the sophisticated fortification systems seen in the Maratha heartland. Hill forts, coastal fortresses, and island strongholds - hallmarks of Maratha military architecture - found their urban counterparts in Meerut's cityscape. The Marathas excelled in adapting their defensive structures to the local terrain, a skill honed in the varied landscapes of the Deccan and now applied to the plains of North India.

Perhaps the most striking feature of Maratha military urbanism was its network of subterranean granaries. These underground storehouses, strategically dispersed throughout the city, ensured a steady supply of provisions even during prolonged sieges. The granaries were engineering marvels, designed to keep grains dry and pest-free for extended periods, a testament to the Marathas' foresight in urban planning with military considerations.

The Marathas also revolutionized Meerut's equestrian infrastructure. Recognizing the importance of cavalry in their military doctrine, they established extensive horse breeding pastures on the outskirts of the city. These pastures not only supplied mounts for the army but also became centers of equestrian excellence, where the famed Maratha light cavalry honed their skills. The layout of these pastures was carefully integrated into the city's defensive perimeter, serving as both a military asset and a buffer zone against potential invaders.

In the heart of Meerut, the Marathas established a cannon foundry, a symbol of their commitment to technological advancement. This foundry, located in the Suraj Kund area, became a hub of innovation, producing artillery that could rival European standards. The presence of this foundry transformed Meerut into a center of military-industrial production, attracting skilled artisans and engineers from across the subcontinent.

The Maratha influence on Meerut's urban fabric went beyond military considerations. They introduced a sophisticated water management system, with tanks and step-wells strategically placed throughout the city. These structures, while primarily serving civic needs, were also integrated into the city's defensive network, ensuring water supply during times of conflict.

As we walk through modern Meerut, echoes of this Maratha military urbanism still resonate. The layout of old neighborhoods, the placement of temples, and the remnants of fortifications all bear witness to an era when city planning was inextricably linked with military strategy. The Maratha legacy in Meerut stands as a testament to their vision - a vision that saw cities not just as places to be defended, but as living, breathing organisms that could be shaped to serve both martial and civic purposes.

This chapter of Meerut's history, often overshadowed by more recent events, deserves recognition for its profound impact on the city's development. The Maratha military urbanism was more than a series of fortifications; it was a comprehensive approach to city-building that balanced security with prosperity, leaving an enduring legacy that continues to shape Meerut's urban landscape to this day.

Colonial Crucible
(1803-1947)

THE SPARK THAT LIT THE INFERNO: MEERUT, MAY 10, 1857

As dusk descended over Meerut on the fateful evening of May 10, 1857, an ominous silence settled over the vast British cantonment. The sprawling military enclave—one of the most significant British strongholds in India—was home to over 2,300 Indian sepoys and 2,000 British officers and soldiers. Its meticulously structured barracks, parade grounds, and armories had been designed for order, discipline, and above all, control. Yet, within these very walls, an uncontainable force was about to be unleashed, a force that would shake the foundations of British rule in India.

For months, resentment had simmered among the Indian soldiers. Years of discrimination, pay disparities, and racial arrogance had bred deep-seated grievances, but it was the introduction of the infamous new cartridges—allegedly greased with cow and pig fat—that became the final provocation. The issue cut deep, offending both Hindu and Muslim sepoys at their core beliefs. The British response to their protest was swift and ruthless: 85 men from the 3rd Bengal Light Cavalry were court-martialed, stripped of their ranks, shackled in iron chains, and sentenced to harsh imprisonment. The indignity of this punishment sent a shockwave through the ranks, a humiliation that could not be ignored.

That evening, as the sun dipped below the horizon, a deceptive calm hung over the cantonment. The oppressive heat of the day gave way to the cool of twilight, but the air was thick with anticipation, charged with an unspoken but shared resolve. Then, suddenly, the quiet shattered. A deafening cry of defiance tore through the air as the imprisoned sepoys broke free from their chains, their rage erupting like a long-dormant volcano.

From the barracks of the 3rd Bengal Light Cavalry, the rebellion spread like wildfire. The disciplined ranks of the 11th and 20th Native Infantry regiments dissolved into a surging tide of mutineers. What had moments ago been a structured military cantonment was now a battleground, where the rigid hierarchy of colonial rule crumbled under the force of raw fury.

The sepoys, intimately familiar with the cantonment's labyrinthine layout, moved swiftly. Between 5:00 PM and 7:00 PM, they stormed the main arsenal, seizing rifles, muskets, and ammunition. The very weapons the British had used to enforce their dominion now turned against them. Gunfire crackled through the night, mingling with the panicked shouts of officers caught off guard. The flames of rebellion burned through the regimented order of the British military establishment, transforming trained soldiers into insurgents with a singular cause.

By 8:00 PM, the revolt had surged beyond the cantonment's confines, spilling into Meerut's civilian quarters like a tidal wave. The bustling bazaar, usually alive with merchants and traders, became a war zone. British officers, caught unarmed in the narrow alleys, were surrounded by emboldened crowds—civilians who had long borne the weight of colonial oppression. Some tried to escape; others met swift and brutal ends. The streets, so often filled with the hum of commerce, now reverberated with the sound of war cries and the clash of steel against steel.

In the Muslim quarters of Meerut, the uprising gained its fiercest momentum. The grievances of the community, simmering under years of British neglect and discrimination, erupted with force. Meanwhile, neighborhoods housing British sympathizers or government officials remained eerily silent, their doors bolted, their occupants cowering in fear of the storm outside.

As the night wore on, the insurgents did not merely revel in their victory; they strategized. By 10:00 PM, a clear path had emerged—a march toward Delhi. The rebels knew that Meerut's uprising, no matter how fierce, would remain an isolated incident unless it became part of a larger, unified movement. Delhi, the seat of the once-mighty Mughal Empire, was more than a geographical target—it was a symbol. A rallying point. A place where the rebellion could be transformed into a full-fledged war for liberation.

As dawn broke on May 11, the city awoke to the grim aftermath of a night of blood and fire. The once-imposing British officers' quarters now stood in eerie devastation, their inhabitants either slain or fled. Smoke curled from buildings set ablaze in the frenzy of the night. The cantonment—once the embodiment of British military dominance—was now a testament to defiance, a battlefield stained with the first real challenge to colonial rule.

Beyond Meerut, the roads leading to Delhi thrummed with movement. Rebels, emboldened by their success, pressed forward, their ranks swelling with each passing mile. Civilians, fearing the inevitable British retaliation, scattered—some fleeing for safety, others swept into the momentum of revolution. The British, though momentarily stunned, would soon regroup, setting the stage for a brutal and prolonged conflict.

The events of May 10, 1857, were more than just the opening act of an insurrection. They marked the beginning of what would later be recognized as India's First War of Independence. The sepoys and civilians who rose up that night were not merely rebels—they were the first torchbearers of a long and arduous struggle that would, decades later, culminate in the end of British rule.

This was not just a battle; it was a reckoning. A moment in history when ordinary men and women, bound by shared suffering and an unyielding thirst for justice, took their fate into their own hands. Their actions that night in Meerut sent tremors through the corridors of power, not just in India but in the distant halls of the British Parliament. It was the beginning of an empire's unraveling, the first whisper of a storm that would ultimately sweep colonial rule into the annals of history.

And it all began on a warm, restless night in Meerut, under a sky heavy with the weight of revolution.

CHAPTER SEVEN

INDUSTRIAL GENESIS: VICTORIAN INFRASTRUCTURE

The industrial transformation of Meerut during the Victorian era was nothing short of a revolution, reshaping the city's economic and social fabric in ways that continue to reverberate to this day. Between 1891 and 1931, the once-sleepy cantonment town witnessed an extraordinary surge in factory permits, ushering in an era of rapid industrialization that positioned Meerut as a key manufacturing and commercial hub in northern India. This metamorphosis was driven by advancements in transportation, cutting-edge technological innovations, and the arrival of electricity—each factor interwoven into the city's evolving economic landscape.

One of the most significant milestones in this industrial evolution was the establishment of Schnabel & Co's leather tannery, a pioneering enterprise that signaled Meerut's growing dominance in the leather industry. Founded in the late 19th century, the tannery distinguished itself through its adoption of chromium salt tanning, a revolutionary process that dramatically enhanced the durability and flexibility of leather. Unlike the traditional vegetable tanning method, which required weeks of processing, chromium tanning cut production time to mere days, making Meerut's leather products more competitive in both domestic and global markets.

The impact was profound. By the early 1900s, Meerut had become a leading supplier of high-quality leather goods, catering to growing demand from British military units stationed across India as well as European markets. The tannery's success laid the foundation for Meerut's emergence as a major center for sports goods manufacturing, particularly in the production of leather-based items such as cricket balls, footballs, and boxing gloves.

A critical factor that accelerated Meerut's industrial ascent was the introduction of the narrow-gauge railway, a game-changing development that connected the city to Delhi, Saharanpur, and beyond. This new transportation network, completed in phases during the late 19th and early 20th centuries, dramatically improved the movement of raw materials and finished goods, integrating Meerut into the broader economy of British India.

The impact of the railway was particularly visible in the sugar industry, which had already taken root in the region. By 1905, Meerut had several fully operational sugar mills, benefiting from the railway's ability to transport sugarcane from rural farms to processing units at unprecedented speeds. This logistical advantage enabled Meerut's sugar output to increase by nearly 40% between 1900 and 1920, strengthening its position as a key player in India's sugar economy.

Furthermore, the railway provided a crucial lifeline for the city's scissors and metalworking industries, which had long been renowned for their craftsmanship. Traditionally confined to local markets, these goods now found their way to traders and buyers in cities as far away as Calcutta, Bombay, and Madras, cementing Meerut's reputation as a center for precision metalwork.

While the railway had provided the means to expand, the arrival of electricity in 1931 was the final piece of the puzzle that propelled Meerut into full-fledged industrial modernity. Electrification was not a haphazard process but a meticulously planned initiative designed to support the city's fastest-growing industries. The first areas to receive power were those hosting tanneries, sugar mills, and metal workshops, ensuring that the city's economic backbone could operate with greater efficiency and scale.

The introduction of electric power transformed small-scale industries, particularly in sports goods manufacturing. With continuous access to machinery, production lines operated longer hours, output increased significantly, and the quality of manufactured goods improved. The availability of reliable electricity also attracted skilled artisans and entrepreneurs from neighboring regions, expanding the labor force and introducing new industrial techniques that would set Meerut apart from other emerging manufacturing hubs.

Between 1931 and 1940, the number of industrial units in Meerut increased by over 60%, with the greatest expansion seen in leather processing, sugar refining, and small-scale metal industries. By the eve of India's independence, Meerut had firmly established itself as a vibrant industrial powerhouse, no longer just a cantonment town but a city with an economic identity of its own.

Reflecting on this transformative period, it is evident that Meerut's modern industrial identity was forged in these Victorian years. The combination of innovative chemical processes, enhanced transportation infrastructure, and electrification set the stage for the city's sustained economic growth. The same industries that flourished in the late 19th and early 20th centuries—leather, metalwork, sugar, and sports goods—continue to be key pillars of Meerut's economy today.

As Meerut now stands on the brink of another industrial leap, with projects such as the Eastern Dedicated Freight Corridor and expanding logistics networks poised to boost trade, we can trace the roots of its industrial prowess back to these pivotal decades. The legacy of Victorian-era investments continues to shape the city's economic destiny, proving that the seeds of progress planted over a century ago remain vital to its future growth.

Post-Independence Evolution

CHAPTER EIGHT

PARTITION'S DEMOGRAPHIC SHOCKWAVES

The Partition of India in 1947 sent seismic waves across the subcontinent, and Meerut found itself at the epicenter of a demographic upheaval that would forever alter its social fabric. In the span of just four years, from 1947 to 1951, Meerut experienced a population explosion that would challenge its infrastructure, reshape its neighborhoods, and transform its cultural landscape.

As the dust settled on the newly drawn borders, Meerut's population swelled from a modest 82,000 to a staggering 137,000 – a surge of over 67% that would strain the city's resources to their breaking point. Refugee camps sprouted like mushrooms on the outskirts of the city, their canvas tents and makeshift shelters becoming temporary homes for thousands fleeing the violence and uncertainty of Partition. These camps, once thought to be temporary, became the crucibles from which new communities would emerge, forever changing Meerut's demographic makeup.

The linguistic tapestry of Meerut, once dominated by Hindi and Urdu, began to interweave with the dialects of Punjab and Sindh as refugees settled into newly formed mohallas. These neighborhoods, often named after the hometowns left behind, became microcosms of the lands from which their residents had fled. Punjabi Lane, Sindhi Colony, and Multani Chowk emerged as testaments to the resilience of those who had lost everything but their mother tongue. The narrow streets echoed with unfamiliar cadences, as shopkeepers and neighbors navigated this new linguistic landscape, creating a unique blend of dialects that would become Meerut's own.

Perhaps nowhere was the impact of this demographic shift more keenly felt than in Meerut's famed metalcraft guilds. For centuries, these artisans had passed down their skills from father to son, their workshops humming with the rhythms of tradition. Now, they found themselves facing an influx of refugee craftsmen, bringing with them techniques and designs from Lahore, Peshawar, and beyond. The collision of these artistic traditions sparked a renaissance in Meerut's metalwork industry. Punjabi koftgari (gold inlay work) merged with local brass casting techniques, giving birth to new forms that would soon find their way to markets across India and beyond.

As the refugee camps slowly emptied and their residents integrated into the city proper, Meerut's economy underwent a transformation. The influx of skilled laborers and entrepreneurs from West Punjab invigorated industries ranging from textiles to sports goods manufacturing. The city's famous scissors industry, in particular, benefited from the arrival of master craftsmen from Sialkot, whose expertise in surgical instrument production would elevate Meerut's reputation on the global stage.

Yet, this rapid growth came at a cost. The strain on Meerut's infrastructure was immense, with water scarcity and sanitation issues plaguing the newly formed neighborhoods. The city's literacy rate, which had been steadily climbing, saw a temporary dip as the education system struggled to accommodate the influx of refugee children. These challenges would shape Meerut's development priorities for decades to come, spurring investments in public works and education that would lay the foundation for the city's future growth.

As we look back on this tumultuous period in Meerut's history, we see not just a demographic shift, but a testament to human resilience. The refugees who arrived with little more than the clothes on their backs would go on to become integral threads in the fabric of Meerut's society, their stories of loss and renewal woven into the very streets they now called home. The Partition may have redrawn the map of India, but it was in cities like Meerut that the true work of healing and rebuilding would unfold, one mohalla at a time.

CHAPTER NINE

SPORTS GOODS CLUSTER: AN INDUSTRIAL ECOSYSTEM

In the heart of Uttar Pradesh, Meerut's sports goods cluster stands as a testament to industrial ingenuity and resilience. This vibrant ecosystem, comprising over 3,500 units and employing upwards of 70,000 workers, has woven itself into the very fabric of the city's identity. The cluster's annual production, valued at a staggering Rs. 200 crores, reverberates through the local economy, with its influence extending far beyond Meerut's boundaries to contribute a quarter of India's sports goods exports.

The story of Meerut's sports manufacturing prowess begins on the fertile floodplains of the Yamuna River. Here, in the rich alluvial soil, grows the raw material that forms the backbone of Meerut's most iconic product: the cricket bat. The English willow and Kashmir willow, cultivated in these plains, are harvested and carefully selected by master craftsmen who can discern the potential for a match-winning six in a single glance at the grain. This intimate connection between the land and the final product has been a cornerstone of Meerut's success, ensuring a steady supply of high-quality raw materials that have made the city's bats the choice of international cricket stars like Virat Kohli and MS Dhoni.

The 1970s marked a pivotal moment in the cluster's evolution, as Meerut's manufacturers pioneered innovative export procedures that would catapult their products onto the global stage. Companies like Sanspareils Greenlands, with roots tracing back to pre-partition Sialkot, led the charge in developing international markets. Their success story is emblematic of the cluster's adaptability, transitioning from a 100% export-oriented model to cultivating a robust domestic market while maintaining their global presence. This period of innovation laid the groundwork for Meerut's current status as a hub for international sports brands, with giants like Adidas and Puma sourcing their cricket equipment from the city's skilled artisans.

In recent years, the cluster has embraced technological advancements with the same fervor that characterized its earlier innovations. The advent of robotics in cricket kit manufacturing represents a quantum leap for Meerut's sports goods industry. Heega Sports stands at the forefront of this revolution, developing AI-powered cricket bats that promise to be the "cheapest in the market". This fusion of traditional craftsmanship with cutting-edge technology exemplifies Meerut's ability to evolve while maintaining its core strengths. The smart cricket bats, equipped with sensors and AI capabilities, are poised to revolutionize not only the manufacturing process but also player training and performance analysis.

As Meerut's sports goods cluster looks to the future, it faces both challenges and opportunities. The need for technological upgrades, improved infrastructure, and easier access to finance looms large. Yet, the cluster's inherent strengths—its concentration of manufacturers within a 10-kilometer radius, a supportive ecosystem, and a reputation for quality—position it well for continued growth. The vision of a trillion-dollar economy for Uttar Pradesh, championed by Chief Minister Yogi Adityanath, offers a tantalizing glimpse of the potential that lies ahead for Meerut's sports goods industry.

In this dynamic landscape, logistics players like Allcargo Gati are stepping up to address the supply chain challenges faced by the cluster. By expanding their reach and introducing sustainable transportation solutions, they are helping to streamline operations and enhance delivery speeds, crucial factors in meeting the growing global demand for Meerut's sports goods.

From the Yamuna's floodplains to the cricket pitches of international stadiums, from handcrafted willows to AI-enhanced bats, Meerut's sports goods cluster continues to evolve, innovate, and inspire. It stands as a shining example of how traditional skills, coupled with modern technology and an entrepreneurial spirit, can create an industrial ecosystem that not only survives but thrives in the face of global competition.

Contemporary Urban Dynamics

CHAPTER TEN

TRANSPORTATION NEUROSIS: A MOBILITY CRISIS

Beneath the shadow of ancient monuments and the glare of neon signs, Meerut pulsates with a paradoxical heartbeat - a city simultaneously surging forward and grinding to a halt. This vibrant nexus of Uttar Pradesh finds itself ensnared in a transportation tangle that threatens to strangle its very lifeblood. The city's arteries, once flowing freely with the rhythms of life, now choke on the metallic congestion of 21st century progress, a stark emblem of India's urban growing pains. Meerut's mobility crisis, a Gordian knot of gridlock, smog, and crumbling infrastructure, has reached a critical mass, crying out for visionary solutions and immediate action.

A meticulous analysis of 14-hour traffic camera footage reveals a city in the throes of mobility crisis. From the crack of dawn to the late hours of night, Meerut's roads pulsate with an ever-increasing volume of vehicles. The footage paints a stark picture: during peak hours, the average speed on major arteries plummets to a mere 15 km/h, transforming what should be short commutes into arduous journeys.

The root of this crisis lies in the explosive growth of vehicle ownership, a trend that has far outpaced the city's ability to expand its road network. Data from the Regional Transport Office (RTO) in Meerut tells a sobering tale. Between 2020 and 2025, the number of registered vehicles in the city has surged by an astounding 40%, while road capacity has increased by a mere 5%. This stark disparity has created a perfect storm of congestion, with two-wheelers and cars jostling for space on roads designed for a fraction of the current traffic volume.

Yet, amidst this chaos, a glimmer of hope emerges in the form of the Meerut Metro project. As of January 2025, trial runs have commenced on the metro line connecting Meerut South to Meerut Central, marking a significant milestone in the city's quest for sustainable urban mobility. The Metro, with its promise of seamless connectivity and reduced travel times, represents more than just a new mode of transport; it embodies the aspirations of a city yearning to break free from the shackles of its transportation woes.

The integration of the Meerut Metro with the Namo Bharat Rapid Rail Transit System (RRTS) at key stations heralds a new era of multimodal transportation for the city. This innovative approach, featuring stations with dual platforms to accommodate both metro and rapid rail services, is set to revolutionize the way Meerut's residents navigate their urban landscape. The potential impact is profound: Partapur, a pivotal suburb of Meerut and a thriving industrial, commercial, and residential hub, stands to benefit immensely. Strategically located along the Delhi-Meerut corridor, Partapur serves as both the city's southern gateway and a critical transit point for daily commuters and goods transport. With its industrial estates, educational institutions, and burgeoning housing projects, the area has long struggled with congestion and inadequate public transport. Now, commuters from Partapur could soon find themselves whisked away to Delhi with unprecedented ease, bypassing the choked highways and gridlocked intersections that have long plagued inter-city travel. As a key link between Meerut's economic core and the larger National Capital Region (NCR), Partapur's integration into the metro and rapid rail network marks a transformative step towards seamless, high-speed connectivity, promising economic growth and enhanced urban mobility..

However, the road to mobility salvation is fraught with challenges. The implementation of advanced Intelligent Transport Systems (ITS) along the Delhi-Meerut Expressway, while promising, highlights the complexity of modernizing urban transportation. The deployment of AI-powered Automatic License Plate Recognition (ALPR) technology and sophisticated vehicle classification systems offers a glimpse into the future of traffic management. Yet, these technological marvels must contend with the harsh realities of Meerut's existing infrastructure and the deeply ingrained habits of its road users.

As Meerut stands on the precipice of transformation, the question remains: can the city overcome its transportation neurosis and emerge as a model of urban mobility? The answer lies not just in the steel tracks of the metro or the algorithms of traffic management systems, but in the collective will of its citizens and policymakers to embrace change. The coming years will be crucial, as Meerut navigates the delicate balance between accommodating its burgeoning vehicle population and fostering a sustainable, multimodal transportation ecosystem.

In this unfolding drama of urban evolution, Meerut's transportation crisis serves as both a cautionary tale and a call to action for cities across India. As the metro trains begin their tentative journeys and smart traffic systems flicker to life, the city stands at the threshold of a new era. The path forward is clear, if challenging: to weave together the threads of technology, infrastructure, and human behavior into a tapestry of urban mobility that can withstand the pressures of growth while enhancing the quality of life for all its residents.

CHAPTER ELEVEN

EDUCATIONAL INFRASTRUCTURE PARADOX

Amidst the bustling streets and ancient monuments of Meerut, a city that has witnessed the ebb and flow of civilizations since the Indus Valley era, a stark educational paradox unfolds. This historical hub in Uttar Pradesh, known for its pivotal role in India's First War of Independence in 1857 and its thriving industries, now finds itself at the crossroads of an educational conundrum that mirrors the challenges faced by many emerging urban centers across the nation.

Meerut's skyline is dotted with the imposing structures of 17 engineering colleges, their campuses buzzing with the energy of young minds eager to carve their place in India's burgeoning tech industry. Each year, these institutions collectively unleash a torrent of 8,400 fresh graduates into the job market, their degrees clutched tightly in hand and dreams of innovation and progress burning brightly in their eyes. Among them, the Meerut Institute of Engineering and Technology (MIET) stands tall, ranked as the 4th best engineering college in Uttar Pradesh by AKTU. With an impressive 80% placement rate, MIET serves as a beacon of academic promise, sending its students to top companies such as Infosys, TCS, Wipro, and HCL.

Yet, beneath this veneer of academic prosperity lies a stark reality that threatens to undermine the very foundations of Meerut's educational ambitions. The city grapples with a staggering 43% skilled labor migration rate, a figure that casts a long shadow over the promises of local educational institutions. This exodus of talent speaks volumes about the disconnect between the skills imparted within Meerut's hallowed halls of learning and the economic realities that await graduates beyond the campus gates. The city finds itself in the unenviable position of being a net exporter of talent, its brightest minds seeking fortunes in the glittering metropolises of Delhi, Mumbai, Bengaluru, and Hyderabad. According to a 2021 study, over 60% of Meerut's engineering graduates leave the city in search of higher salaries, better job prospects, and greater industry exposure, leaving behind a local economy starved of skilled professionals.

In a curious twist of fate, as Meerut's homegrown talent scatters to the winds, the city has witnessed a proliferation of corporate training centers, hoping to fill the void. These institutions, ranging from behemoths like Sigma Classes to niche providers like Get Fit Yoga Club, have sprung up like mushrooms after a monsoon rain. They offer a smorgasbord of courses, from SSC, banking, and railway exam coaching to soft skills training, personality development, and niche certifications. Their rapid rise underscores the growing realization that traditional academic degrees alone are often insufficient to meet the practical demands of modern employers. These training centers represent a booming Rs. 300-crore industry in Meerut, highlighting the growing market for supplementary education and skill enhancement.

The paradox deepens when one considers the influx of students and job seekers from neighboring districts like Bulandshahr, Aligarh, Muzaffarnagar, and Baghpat, drawn to Meerut's reputation as an educational hub. These newcomers, often from rural backgrounds, enter a complex ecosystem of academic institutions, coaching centers, and job placement agencies, each promising a pathway to success in an increasingly competitive market. This migration fuels Meerut's urban sprawl, stretching its resources thin as its population, currently hovering around 3.9 million, continues to grow. The city's infrastructure, particularly in housing, transportation, and public utilities, struggles to keep pace with the educational boom.

As Meerut stands on the precipice of a new era, with ambitious projects like the Delhi-Meerut Expressway, the Rapid Rail Transit System (RRTS), and proposed IT parks promising to further integrate it into the National Capital Region (NCR), a pivotal question looms large: Can the city reconcile its role as an educational powerhouse with the harsh realities of its labor market? The answer lies not just in the lecture halls and laboratories of its engineering colleges, but in the boardrooms of local industries, the corridors of power in Lucknow, and the aspirations of its youth.

Meerut's industrial sector, despite its historical strengths in sports goods, sugar, and handloom industries, has yet to fully capitalize on its academic output. While the city boasts a Rs. 4,000-crore sports manufacturing industry, an Rs. 3,500-crore sugar economy, and a Rs. 1,200-crore handloom sector, these industries have not evolved at the pace needed to absorb the wave of engineering graduates. The disconnect between Meerut's academic strengths and its industrial ecosystem continues to fuel the migration dilemma.

The educational infrastructure paradox of Meerut serves as a microcosm of India's broader challenges in aligning its vast human capital with the demands of a rapidly evolving global economy. As Meerut grapples with this conundrum, it may yet emerge as a model for how emerging urban centers can bridge the gap between education and employment, stemming the tide of migration and fostering sustainable, locally-driven economic growth.

The story of Meerut's educational journey is far from over; indeed, it may be that the most important chapters are yet to be written. With strategic investments in local industry, incubation centers for startups, and stronger industry-academia collaborations, Meerut has the potential to transform from a city that exports talent to one that retains, nurtures, and thrives on it.

Future Horizons (2025-2047)

CHAPTER TWELVE

ZONAL DEVELOPMENT PLAN 2041: CRITICAL APPRAISAL

As Meerut stands on the cusp of a new era, the Zonal Development Plan 2041 emerges as a visionary blueprint for the city's future, weaving together cutting-edge technology, environmental stewardship, and cultural preservation. At the heart of this ambitious plan lies a series of groundbreaking interventions that promise to transform Meerut into a model of sustainable urban development for the 21st century.

Perhaps the most revolutionary aspect of the plan is its innovative approach to water management through the creation of stormwater highways. These are not mere drainage systems, but sophisticated networks designed to capture, filter, and channel rainwater directly into Meerut's depleted aquifers. Drawing inspiration from ancient water harvesting techniques and marrying them with modern engineering, these stormwater highways will crisscross the city, turning every monsoon into an opportunity for groundwater replenishment. The plan envisions the construction of over 150 basin recharge structures and an equal number of river recharge pits along the Yamuna and Hindon floodplains, with the potential to augment groundwater storage by a staggering 420 million cubic meters. This ambitious project not only addresses Meerut's chronic water scarcity but also offers a sustainable solution to urban flooding, transforming a perennial challenge into a valuable resource.

In a bold move to revolutionize urban agriculture, the Zonal Development Plan mandates the integration of vertical farming systems into new building codes. This forward-thinking approach recognizes the critical need to balance urban growth with food security and environmental sustainability. Under the new regulations, developers will be required to allocate a percentage of built-up area for hydroponic and aeroponic farming systems, effectively turning Meerut's skyline into a verdant tapestry of productive green spaces. These vertical farms, nestled within the city's architectural fabric, promise to reduce food miles, enhance urban biodiversity, and create new employment opportunities in high-tech agriculture. The plan draws inspiration from successful urban farming initiatives worldwide, adapting them to Meerut's unique climatic and cultural context.

Perhaps the most intriguing aspect of the Zonal Development Plan is its embrace of artificial intelligence in the service of heritage conservation. Meerut, with its rich tapestry of historical sites spanning millennia, from

Harappan-era settlements to Mughal monuments, faces the constant challenge of balancing preservation with progress. The plan introduces an AI-powered monitoring system that will use a network of sensors, drones, and satellite imagery to create a real-time digital twin of Meerut's heritage sites. This sophisticated system will not only alert conservationists to potential threats but also predict future degradation patterns, allowing for proactive intervention. By harnessing the power of machine learning algorithms, Meerut aims to become a pioneer in smart heritage management, ensuring that its historical treasures endure for generations to come.

As Meerut embarks on this ambitious journey towards 2041, the Zonal Development Plan stands as a testament to the city's commitment to innovation and sustainability. However, the path ahead is not without challenges. The successful implementation of these interventions will require not only significant investment but also a paradigm shift in urban governance and citizen participation. The stormwater highways, while promising, will demand careful integration with existing infrastructure and potential disruption during construction. The vertical farming mandate, revolutionary as it is, may face resistance from traditional developers and will necessitate new skills and technologies in the construction sector. Similarly, the AI-powered heritage conservation system will require robust data protection measures and ongoing technological upgrades to remain effective.

Yet, as Meerut faces the twin pressures of rapid urbanization and climate change, the Zonal Development Plan 2041 offers a beacon of hope. It envisions a city where ancient wisdom and cutting-edge technology coalesce, where every raindrop is treasured, every building contributes to food security, and every historical artifact is vigilantly protected. As this plan unfolds over the coming decades, Meerut stands poised to redefine what it means to be a truly smart and sustainable city in the heart of India.

CHAPTER THIRTEEN

GANGA-JAMUNA SMART ECOTONE PROJECT

In the heart of Uttar Pradesh, where ancient rivers whisper tales of civilizations past, Meerut is poised to write a new chapter in its storied history. The Ganga-Jamuna Smart Ecotone Project rises like a phoenix from the banks of its twin lifelines, promising to weave a tapestry of innovation and nature that will redefine urban living. This audacious vision seeks to metamorphose the once-neglected riverfront into a pulsating, sustainable ecosystem where cutting-edge technology dances in harmony with the timeless rhythms of nature.

At the heart of this transformative project lies an innovative approach to tackling one of Meerut's most pressing environmental challenges: industrial pollution. The city's waterways, long burdened by the effluent of its bustling industrial sector, are set to undergo a remarkable metamorphosis through the implementation of mycoremediation wetlands. These living filtration systems harness the power of fungi to break down complex pollutants, transforming toxic waste into harmless byproducts. Stretching along the riverbanks, these wetlands will not only purify water but also create a vibrant habitat for local flora and fauna, effectively turning a once-blighted area into a biodiversity hotspot.

As visitors stroll along the newly revitalized riverfront, their gaze will be drawn to a shimmering spectacle on the water's surface. Floating solar arrays, resembling a fleet of futuristic lily pads, will harness the sun's energy to power the surrounding eco-district. These innovative installations not only generate clean electricity but also serve multiple ecological functions. By shading the water, they reduce evaporation and algal growth, while their submerged structures provide sanctuary for aquatic life. The gentle hum of these solar islands will be a constant reminder of Meerut's commitment to sustainable energy solutions.

Perhaps the most striking feature of the Smart Ecotone Project is its bold foray into amphibious architecture. Drawing inspiration from successful implementations in the Netherlands and the United Kingdom, Meerut is set to pioneer this flood-resilient building technique in India. The first prototype, a sleek three-story structure on the Ganga's banks, appears to be a conventional building at first glance. However, this architectural marvel conceals a revolutionary secret: the ability to rise and float during flood events. Resting on a buoyant base and guided by vertical posts, the building can ascend up to 2.7 meters, effortlessly adapting to rising water levels. This amphibious design not only ensures the safety of residents but also allows for a harmonious coexistence with the river's natural flood cycles.

As the project unfolds, the Ganga-Jamuna riverfront will be transformed into a living laboratory of sustainable urban development. Pedestrian walkways will wind through the mycoremediation wetlands, offering citizens and visitors alike an immersive educational experience in ecological restoration. The floating solar arrays will become a symbol of Meerut's commitment to renewable energy, inspiring other cities to follow suit. And the amphibious buildings, rising and falling with the ebb and flow of the rivers, will stand as a testament to human ingenuity in the face of climate change.

The Ganga-Jamuna Smart Ecotone Project represents more than just an urban renewal initiative; it is a bold reimagining of how cities can coexist with their natural environments. By embracing the rivers rather than fighting against them, Meerut is positioning itself at the forefront of climate-resilient urban design. As this visionary project takes shape, it promises not only to revitalize the city's waterfront but also to rekindle the deep connection between Meerut's citizens and the sacred rivers that have sustained their civilization for millennia.

Cultural Continuums

CHAPTER FOURTEEN

FOLKTALES OF MEERUT: ECHOES OF ANCIENT WISDOM

Meerut, with its rich historical and cultural heritage, is home to a treasure trove of folktales that have been passed down through generations. These stories, woven into the fabric of local tradition, reflect the city's diverse influences and its connection to ancient Indian mythology. This chapter aims to shed light on some of the more popular folk-tales of Meerut.

Maya Rashtra

One popular folktale revolves around the origin of the city's name.

In the mists of ancient times, when gods and demons walked the earth, there lived a great asura architect named Mayasura. His skill in crafting magnificent structures was unparalleled, and his fame spread far and wide across the land.

One day, Mayasura caught the attention of King Yudhishthira, who was impressed by the asura's architectural prowess. As a gesture of goodwill and recognition of his talents, Yudhishthira granted Mayasura a vast tract of land. Overjoyed with this gift, Mayasura decided to build his capital on this land, naming it "Maya Rashtra" - the kingdom of Maya.

Maya Rashtra flourished under Mayasura's rule, becoming a city of unparalleled beauty and innovation. Its buildings were said to be so intricate and magnificent that they left visitors awestruck, their minds unable to distinguish between reality and illusion. The crown jewel of Maya Rashtra was the grand palace of illusions, known as Maya Sabha, which Mayasura later built for the Pandavas.

As centuries passed, the name of the city evolved, much like the layers of civilization that built upon its foundations. From Maya Rashtra, it became Mairashtra, then transformed to Mai-dant-ka-khera, before finally settling into the name we know today - Meerut.

The legacy of Mayasura lived on not just in the city's name, but also through his daughter, Mandodari. Known for her beauty and virtue, Mandodari became the wife of the great demon king Ravana. Thus, Meerut's connection to the epic Ramayana was forged, linking the city to one of the greatest stories in Hindu mythology.

To this day, the people of Meerut take pride in their city's mythical origins. They say that the spirit of Mayasura's creativity and innovation still infuses the city, inspiring its residents to reach for the stars, much like the asura architect did in those ancient days when he built a kingdom that would stand the test of time.

Nauchandi

Another story that resonates with the locals is tied to the Nauchandi fair, a tradition that has endured for over 350 years. The fair, which began in 1672, is said to have its roots in ancient legends of valor and devotion.

Legend has it that in the 11th century, a young Sufi saint named Hazrat Bale Miyan arrived in Meerut. Though only 12 years old, his wisdom and teachings quickly earned him the name "Bale Miyan," meaning "little scholar." His message of peace and harmony attracted followers from all walks of life.

Across from where Bale Miyan preached stood an ancient temple dedicated to Goddess Chandi, a fierce avatar of Durga. It is said that Mandodari, the virtuous wife of the demon king Ravana, had built this temple in devotion to the goddess.

On a fateful new moon night in 1034 AD, the 19-year-old Bale Miyan was killed by those who opposed his inclusive teachings. As news of his death spread, a great congregation gathered at the site, mourning the loss of the beloved saint.

In the years that followed, a curious phenomenon began to unfold. During the Navratri festival, devotees flocking to the Chandi temple would also pay their respects at Bale Miyan's tomb. Similarly, those visiting the Sufi saint's resting place would offer prayers at the goddess's shrine. This spontaneous mingling of faiths gave birth to a unique celebration.

As the annual gathering grew over centuries, attracting traders, performers, and devotees, it evolved into the Nauchandi Mela—a name blending nau (nine) and Chandi (goddess), referencing its roots in a nine-day Hindu festival honoring Goddess Durga. By the 19th century, the event had become a symbol of communal harmony, coinciding with the urs of Sufi saint Bale Miyan. In 1880, the British administration formally recognized the fair, streamlining its management.

Today, the Nauchandi Mela stands as a symbol of unity, where the qawwalis sung at Bale Miyan's dargah blend seamlessly with the bhajans from the Chandi temple. It is a place where the aroma of sacred incense mingles with the enticing scents of local delicacies like nan khatai and halwa paratha.

As the fair continues to draw thousands each year, it serves as a reminder of the enduring power of faith and the strength found in diversity. The Nauchandi Mela remains a beacon of hope, showing that even in times of division, the spirit of unity can prevail, just as it has in Meerut for nearly a thousand years.

Abu Naala and Abu Lane

In the heart of Meerut lies a tale of ingenuity and foresight, woven into the very fabric of the city's infrastructure. The story of Abu Nala and Abu Lane traces back to the 17th century, during the reign of the Mughal emperors Jahangir and Shah Jahan.

Nawab Abu Muhammad Khan, a distinguished nobleman who held the title of Hazari in the royal court, commanded an impressive force of 1,000 foot soldiers and 800 cavalry. But his true legacy lies not in his military might, but in his visionary contributions to Meerut's development.

In an era when clean water was a precious commodity, Nawab Abu conceived a grand plan to bring fresh drinking water to the city from the Kali Nadi, a tributary of the Ganges originating in the Doon Valley, which has historically played a crucial role in Meerut's water supply and agricultural prosperity. He commissioned the construction of a canal, stretching for miles, to quench the thirst of Meerut's growing population. This ambitious project became known as Abu Nala, named after its creator.

Though the canal never fulfilled its original purpose of bringing drinking water, it found new life as a vital drainage system. Today, Abu Nala serves the city's 3.5 million residents, standing as a testament to Nawab Abu's foresight and the adaptability of his creation.

Alongside the canal, a road emerged, lined with the finest establishments in Meerut. This bustling thoroughfare came to be known as Abu Lane, honoring the man whose vision shaped the city's landscape. Today, Abu Lane is a vibrant market stretching nearly a kilometer, boasting high-end showrooms and serving as the commercial heart of Meerut.

The legacy of Nawab Abu Muhammad Khan extends beyond the canal and the lane. He also erected the famous Kamboh Gate of Meerut fort, which later transformed into the iconic Ghantaghar or clock tower, a landmark that has graced many a Bollywood film.

As centuries passed, the name of Abu Lane evolved, much like the city itself. In 1982, it was officially renamed after Rabindranath Tagore, becoming Ravindrapuri in legal documents. Yet, in the hearts and daily lives of Meerut's residents, it remains Abu Lane, a living tribute to the nobleman who shaped their city.

Today, as Meerut stands at the crossroads of tradition and progress, the tales of Abu Nala and Abu Lane serve as reminders of a visionary past. They are not merely infrastructure or marketplaces, but living legacies of a man who dared to dream of a better future for his city.

Bhole Ki Jhaal

In the golden-hued plains southwest of Meerut, where the Kali Nadi river carves its path through fields of sugarcane and mustard, lies Bhole Ki Jhaal—a place where myth and reality merge like currents in a sacred stream. Known locally as Salawa Dam, this ancient reservoir is more than a feat of engineering; it is a living chronicle of faith, survival, and the enduring bond between a land and its people.

The dam's story begins with a legend whispered through generations. Centuries ago, when the earth cracked under unrelenting drought and crops withered to dust, the desperate prayers of villagers rose to Lord Shiva. Moved by their devotion, the deity—revered here as Bhole Nath, the Innocent One—plunged his trident into the barren soil. From that strike surged a life-giving torrent, birthing the Kali Nadi and transforming the parched earth into a fertile oasis. Today, the waters of Bhole Ki Jhaal still ripple with that divine legacy, their surface reflecting the towering spire of an 18th-century Shiva temple, where incense smoke curls skyward alongside the chants of devotees.

For farmers across 42 villages, these waters are the pulse of survival. Each dawn, irrigation channels fan out from the dam like veins, nourishing over 8,000 hectares of land. Here, the rhythm of life follows the reservoir's ebb and flow—the planting of sugarcane in its moist soil, the golden dance of wheat at harvest, the laughter of children splashing in canals after school. Yet the dam's gifts extend beyond practicality. During Maha Shivratri, its banks swell with over 50,000 pilgrims who come to bathe in waters believed to wash away sins. Mothers dip infants into the reservoir, their laughter mingling with the clang of temple bells, while elders float offerings of marigolds and milk, their faces alight with devotion.

Nature, too, finds refuge here. As winter sun gilds the water's surface, painted storks descend like winged ghosts, their slender legs slicing through the shallows. Sarus cranes—tall as children—stalk the wetlands, their crimson heads bobbing as they court mates. These wetlands, once overlooked, have become a battleground for conservationists fighting to protect this avian haven from the encroaching shadows of pollution.

The dam itself is a silent witness to centuries of human ingenuity. Beneath its modern facade lies a 12th-century marvel—a stepped structure of interlocking bricks and lime mortar, designed by forgotten engineers whose brilliance still baffles experts. British colonizers later reinforced it with sandstone, leaving their own mark on this timeless sentinel. Recent sonar scans have revealed hidden chambers, sparking whispers of buried relics and untold stories.

Come February, the dam transforms. The Shiv-Jhoola Mela erupts in a riot of color and sound—farmers barter heirloom seeds under striped tents, Sufi qawwals duel with bhajan singers, and children clamber onto makeshift Ferris wheels that creak skyward. In a quieter corner, devotees release glistening mahseer fish into the water, a centuries-old ritual of atonement now guarded by ecologists balancing faith with conservation.

Last year, archaeologists scraping at the dam's edges uncovered a trove of medieval shivalingas and Maratha-era coins, treasures now displayed in Meerut's museum. These finds have reignited pride in Bhole Ki Jhaal—not just as a reservoir, but as a keeper of memories.

As the sun sinks behind the dam, painting the sky in hues of saffron and ash, fishermen cast their nets in the same waters where Shiva's trident once struck. Their silhouettes blur with those of pilgrims circling the temple, and herons skimming the shallows. Here, in the twilight, Bhole Ki Jhaal reveals its truth: it is not merely a place, but a promise—a testament to how earth and water, faith and survival, can weave a story that outlasts empires.

The Mint That Flew by Night

On the sweltering night of May 10, 1857, as Meerut's skies simmered with the heat of rebellion, a band of sepoys gathered in the shadow of the **Augarnath Temple**, their faces lit by the flickering light of Shiva's eternal flame. The British garrison had fallen, its officers slain or fled, and the rebels now faced an unexpected dilemma: they had seized the East India Company's treasury, brimming with silver ingots, but no means to mint coins to fund their revolution.

"Without rupees, how will we pay our soldiers?" growled **Rao Kadam Singh**, a hulking Rajput subedar, kicking a chest of unmarked silver. His comrade, **Mohan Singh**, a wiry Sikh artilleryman, spat bitterly: "The British took our lands, our dignity—must we now beg for coins too?"

It was then that **Baba Gulab Das**, the temple's aged priest, emerged from the sanctum, his voice trembling with fervor. "The devotee who dies fighting tyranny attains moksha," he intoned, "but the *revolution* needs more than souls. It needs silver tongues to speak its name across Hindustan." Raising his trishul toward the heavens, he cried: "Light a havan! Let Agni carry our plea to Kailash!"

As the rebels kindled a sacred fire, a strange mist rolled in from the Kali River. Thunder cracked—not from the sky, but from the earth itself. Farmers in nearby **Daurala** later swore they saw a colossal bull with eyes like molten copper galloping westward, its hooves striking sparks that lit the Grand Trunk Road. By dawn, the rebels awoke to a marvel: where the British cavalry stables had stood, there now loomed a minting press, its iron gears still warm, its dies etched with lotus blooms and the Urdu legend *"Sikka-e-Mujahid, Zarb-e-Meerut"* (Coin of the Holy Warrior, Struck at Meerut).

The mint's first coins were no crude imitations. Crafted from 90% pure silver, each rupee bore:

- **Obverse**: A lotus (symbolizing purity) encircled by 108 petals—a sacred Hindu number.
- **Reverse**: A crescent moon and *tulwar* (curved sword), representing Muslim and Sikh allies.
- **Edge**: A clandestine inscription in Brahmi script: *"As long as this coin rings, tyranny shall not reign."*

Local jewelers claimed the dies glowed red-hot without fuel, their metallic scent tinged with sandalwood. By noon, the mint had produced 5,000 rupees, distributed by rebel soldiers who shouted: "Take these! Let the Angrez choke on their own silver!"

When Commissioner William Markham later stormed the mint's ruins (the rebels had destroyed it before retreating), he found bizarre anomalies:

- A half-melted bellows bearing the crest of the **Calcutta Mint**, 1,300 km away.
- Hoofprints in the courtyard clay, measuring 18 inches across—far larger than any bull in India.
- A scrap of Persian verse nailed to a beam: *"When Nandi's breath fans the forge, even Death flees the coins of free men."*

Today, a handful of these rupees survive in private collections, their edges worn smooth by generations of retelling. Folk singers in **Sardhana** still perform the *"Geet-e-Sikka"* (Ballad of the Coins), which claims:
"Each rupee carried Shiva's blessing—for every coin spent, a British cannon misfired!"

Historians confirm rebels minted coins in Meerut using captured silver, likely repurposing tools from the city's thriving jewelry bazaars. Yet, the legend's magic persists: at **St. John's Church**, a weathered stone near the bell tower is said to bear Nandi's hoofprint—a testament to the night a mint flew on the wings of rebellion.

Visitors to Meerut's **Freedom Struggle Museum** can view one of the original Sikka-e-Mujahid coins, its lotus petals worn but defiantly visible—a metallic whisper of a night when faith and fury forged a currency of revolution.

CHAPTER FIFTEEN

LANDMARKS OF LEGACY: MEERUT'S JOURNEY THROUGH TIME

Meerut, a city steeped in history and cultural significance, is a living chronicle of India's past, where every street, monument, and marketplace whispers tales of bygone eras. Nestled in the heart of Uttar Pradesh, Meerut is a fascinating blend of antiquity and modernity, a city where medieval forts stand in the shadow of bustling urban centers. Its landmarks, each an enduring testament to its storied past, offer visitors an unparalleled glimpse into a rich and multifaceted heritage.

One of the most remarkable of these landmarks is the Basilica of Our Lady of Graces in Sardhana, a stunning edifice that embodies Indo-European architectural brilliance. Situated 19 kilometers northwest of Meerut, this

Roman Catholic church, commonly known as the Sardhana Church, stands as an awe-inspiring tribute to faith, artistry, and an extraordinary historical figure—Begum Samru. Born as a Muslim nautch girl, she defied societal norms to become the only Catholic ruler in India, converting to Christianity in 1781 and adopting the name Joanna Nobilis Sombre. A formidable leader and a woman of remarkable acumen, she governed the Principality of Sardhana in the 18th and 19th centuries, amassing both power and wealth.

The construction of this majestic church began either in 1809 or 1820, with conflicting historical records, and was consecrated in 1822, as evidenced by a Latin inscription on its façade. The cost of its construction—a staggering 400,000 rupees at the time—reflected the grand vision of its patron. The church is a magnificent fusion of architectural styles, drawing inspiration from St. Peter's Basilica in Rome, yet incorporating Palladian influences and indigenous elements. Its imposing façade, crowned with three Roman domes and two towering spires, stands as a beacon visible from miles away. The church's surrounding two lakes, formed from excavated mud used in its construction, add to the ethereal beauty of this site.

Inside, the church is an artistic marvel. Its polished marble floors, intricately carved altar, and stunning stained-glass windows transport visitors to another era. In 1834, Pope Gregory XVI designated it as the cathedral of the Apostolic Vicariate of Sardhana, briefly elevating its ecclesiastical stature. Though it lost its cathedral status, the church was later honored in 1961 when Pope John XXIII conferred upon it the rare and prestigious title of Minor Basilica, making it North India's only basilica. Today, it remains not just a religious sanctuary but also an architectural jewel that continues to draw thousands of pilgrims and history enthusiasts alike.

Beyond Sardhana, the heart of Meerut holds another architectural and historical marvel—the St. John's Church. Constructed between 1819 and 1821 under the East India Company, it remains one of the oldest and largest churches in northern India. With its high ceilings, Gothic arches, and sprawling interiors, the church can accommodate over 3,000 worshippers at a time, a testament to its colonial past and the significant British presence in the city. Even today, the church resonates with hymns and prayers, its walls having witnessed the tides of history, including the Revolt of 1857, which began in Meerut and marked the first war of Indian independence.

For those intrigued by Meerut's mythological past, Vidura-ka-Tila, an ancient mound rising 50 to 60 feet, offers a compelling journey into the world of the Mahabharata. According to legend, this site was the hermitage of Vidura, the wise minister of the Kauravas. Believed to be over 5,000 years old, these mounds have drawn historians, archaeologists, and spiritual seekers who come to explore the city's deep-rooted connection with India's epic past.

Meerut is not just a city of antiquity but also a symbol of resistance. The Augharnath Temple (popularly known as Kali Paltan temple), one of the oldest temples in the city, played a pivotal role in India's freedom struggle. It was here, amidst the sanctum's divine energy, that soldiers and revolutionaries secretly plotted the first major uprising against British rule in 1857. The temple, dedicated to Lord Shiva, remains a place of devotion and patriotism, its eternal flame (Akhand Jyoti) burning in honor of the freedom fighters who ignited the flames of revolt.

Meerut's landscape is an eclectic mix of historical and contemporary landmarks. From the Victoria Park, a serene expanse originally built as a British cantonment garden, to the Shahid Smarak, a solemn monument dedicated to the martyrs of 1857, every corner of the city is a reminder of its tumultuous yet fascinating journey.

For those drawn to modern entertainment, Melange Mall in Pallavapuram has emerged as a hub of contemporary shopping, dining, and leisure. However, the city's traditional bazaars—Sadar Bazaar, Lal Kurti, and the shimmering Saraffa Bazaar—continue to thrive, proving that Meerut's commercial pulse remains firmly rooted in its rich past.

In recent years, the city has also embraced sustainability and organic living, with initiatives like OrganiC AaharaM, spearheaded by the Janhit Foundation, leading the charge in promoting organic food and sustainable farming. These efforts are not only catering to the health-conscious population but also putting Meerut on the map as a leader in India's organic revolution.

From the grandeur of Sardhana's Basilica to the revolutionary spirit of Augharnath Temple, from the colonial grandeur of St. John's Church to the mythological whispers of Vidura-ka-Tila, Meerut's landmarks offer a journey through time, inviting visitors to delve into its layered past. It is a city where history is not just preserved in monuments but lives on in its people, traditions, and spirit of progress.

CHAPTER SIXTEEN

MOHALLAS OF MEERUT: A TAPESTRY OF TIME AND TRADITION

Nestled in the heart of Uttar Pradesh, Meerut stands as a city where ancient legacies and modern aspirations merge in a vibrant, evolving urban mosaic. At its core lie the mohallas—intricate neighborhoods that serve as microcosms of the city's cultural, economic, and social landscape. Each mohalla carries with it an identity shaped by centuries of historical events, economic shifts, and communal interactions, making them not just clusters of homes but living chronicles of Meerut's ever-changing story.

The evolution of Meerut's mohallas is inextricably linked to the city's long and often turbulent history. A settlement dating back to the Harappan period, Meerut has been shaped by waves of empires—from the Mauryas and Guptas to the Delhi Sultanate and the Mughals. However, its modern demographic transformation, particularly its religious clustering, has roots in the communal strife that defined much of the 20th century.

Between 1961 and 1982, Meerut witnessed a series of riots that left an indelible mark on its urban fabric. The aftermath of the 1982 riots, in particular, accelerated a phenomenon that sociologists describe as "ghettoization"—a demographic shift where communities increasingly settled within religiously homogeneous neighborhoods. This process led to the consolidation of Hindu-majority areas like Shastri Nagar, known for its organized residential colonies, and Muslim-dominated zones such as Zakir Colony, a bustling, self-sufficient enclave with its own schools, businesses, and cultural institutions.

Beyond these modern transformations, the mohallas of Meerut hold within them layers of history dating back centuries. One of the oldest quarters of the city lies around Jama Masjid, a grand structure built in the 11th century by Mahmud of Ghazni's governor. But long before the mosque stood, this area was a prominent center of Buddhist learning during Emperor Ashoka's reign. Even today, as one navigates its maze-like streets, echoes of different eras resonate—the call to prayer mingles with the sights and sounds of a thriving marketplace where artisans craft intricate zari work, metal goods, and traditional clothing.

In stark contrast, Meerut Cantonment, established by the British in 1803, retains an entirely different character. With its tree-lined avenues, colonial-era bungalows, and the sprawling parade ground, it serves as a reminder of Meerut's pivotal role in India's First War of Independence in 1857. It was here, among the military barracks, that the rebellion against British rule ignited, spreading like wildfire across the country. Today, the cantonment area remains a unique blend of the past and present, home to both military families and civilians who cherish its relative tranquility and well-maintained infrastructure.

Beyond being residential spaces, many of Meerut's mohallas function as epicenters of commerce and craftsmanship. The Suraj Kund Sports Market, for instance, serves as the heartbeat of Meerut's globally renowned sports goods industry. Here, generations of skilled artisans craft cricket bats, hockey sticks, footballs, and athletic gear, supplying not just the Indian market but also exporting to over 100 countries worldwide. Meerut's dominance in this industry has earned it the title of "The Sports City of India."

Elsewhere, the metalwork traditions of the city flourish in mohallas like Sarai Behleem and Bhumiya Ka Pul, where artisans have honed their craft for centuries. The city's brassware, scissors, and swords are still highly sought after, and the echoes of hammers striking metal in these workshops tell a tale of resilience in the face of industrial modernity.

Meerut's mohallas also embody the city's rich religious diversity. Hindu temples, Muslim mosques, Sikh gurudwaras, and Christian churches dot the landscape, often standing in close proximity. One of the best examples of this coexistence is the Nauchandi Fair, a tradition that dates back to 1672. This annual event sees people of all faiths coming together to celebrate, trade, and partake in cultural festivities, reinforcing the spirit of pluralism that has long defined the city.

Yet, this harmony has been tested by social and political fault lines. A telling incident occurred in 2017 when a

Hindu-dominated locality protested against a Muslim family purchasing a house in their neighborhood. Such incidents underscore the ongoing challenges of integration, as Meerut continues to grapple with the push and pull between its historical legacy of coexistence and modern-day anxieties fueled by political and economic factors.

As Meerut expands, the cityscape is undergoing rapid transformation. New residential colonies, commercial complexes, and infrastructure projects like the Delhi-Meerut Expressway and the Rapid Rail Transit System promise to bring economic growth and modernization. These developments are attracting a new wave of professionals and businesses, altering the traditional dynamics of the mohallas.

Despite these advancements, the historic neighborhoods remain the heart and soul of Meerut. Their narrow lanes, ancient havelis, and artisanal workshops continue to tell the story of a city that has thrived through centuries of change. As Meerut marches toward a more cosmopolitan future, its mohallas will likely evolve, yet their essence—deeply rooted in history, craft, and community—will endure.

Meerut's mohallas are more than just places; they are living, breathing narratives of survival, adaptation, and identity. In their past lies the story of India's evolving urban landscape, and in their future, perhaps, a vision of what that landscape can become.

BAZAARS OF MEERUT: WHERE HISTORY AND COMMERCE CONVERGE

In the heart of Uttar Pradesh, where history and modernity converge in an intricate dance, lie the bustling bazaars of Meerut—a mesmerizing mosaic of colors, sounds, and scents that have evolved over centuries. These markets, alive with the energy of commerce and tradition, serve as both the lifeblood of the city's economy and a window into its soul. Each lane, every storefront, and every vendor tells a story—of ancient trades, colonial legacies, and an ever-adapting present shaped by shifting consumer habits and global influences.

At the very nucleus of Meerut's commercial vibrancy stands Sadar Bazaar, a marketplace that dates back to the British colonial era. Originally established to cater to the

British soldiers stationed in the Meerut Cantonment, this bazaar has transformed into a shopping mecca that pulsates with life. Its narrow, winding lanes are lined with an eclectic mix of shops selling everything from exquisite handicrafts and traditional garments to modern electronics and trendy fashion accessories. A walk through Sadar Bazaar is a sensory overload—hawkers calling out their wares, the aroma of fresh street food wafting through the air, and the ceaseless chatter of eager customers bargaining for the best deals. This bazaar, once a necessity for soldiers avoiding long treks into the city, has now cemented itself as an indispensable shopping hub for residents from all walks of life.

As one delves deeper into the labyrinth of Meerut's marketplaces, the dazzling brilliance of Saraffa Bazaar unfolds—a gold and silver market that gleams like a treasure chest under the sun. Meerut, often regarded as one of India's premier hubs for jewelry craftsmanship, boasts more than 40 BIS Hallmark-certified gold showrooms concentrated in this area alone. Here, skilled artisans, whose craft has been honed over generations, meticulously design jewelry that seamlessly blends traditional motifs with contemporary elegance. Customers navigate through shimmering displays of necklaces, bangles, and rings, each piece a testament to the city's legacy as a center for fine jewelry. The rhythmic clang of goldsmiths at work is a reminder that, beyond the dazzling storefronts, an ancient craft continues to thrive in the heart of this historic marketplace.

For the food connoisseur, no visit to Meerut's bazaars is complete without stepping into Budhana Gate Market, a gastronomic paradise where the city's rich culinary heritage comes alive. This street-food haven is an explosion of flavors, offering an irresistible array of local delicacies that have stood the test of time. The air is thick with the scent of spiced kebabs sizzling over open flames, the sweet, syrupy aroma of freshly made jalebis, and the comforting warmth of piping-hot kachoris. Here, generations-old eateries serve dishes that have been perfected through time-honored family recipes, drawing food lovers from across the city. Each bite is not just a taste—it is an experience, a connection to Meerut's past and present.

Venturing into Suraj Kund Market, one encounters a different side of Meerut—its prowess as the "Sports City of India." This bustling commercial hub is the epicenter of Meerut's world-renowned sports goods industry, where workshops and retail stores overflow with cricket bats, hockey sticks, footballs, and other sporting equipment. The leather artisans of Suraj Kund, who have long mastered the delicate balance between durability and precision, supply sports gear to national and international markets alike. It is in these workshops that raw materials are transformed into the very cricket bats that have graced some of the most prestigious stadiums in the world. The rhythmic tapping of wood being carved, the steady hum of sewing machines stitching leather, and the sight of craftsmen meticulously perfecting their products encapsulate the spirit of Meerut's industriousness.

Stepping into the Lal Kurti Market, one is transported to an era when British red-coated soldiers roamed the streets of Meerut. This market, whose name literally translates to "Red Coat" in reference to the British Indian Army's uniforms, was once a supplier of military gear. Today, it has evolved into a thriving center for premium leather goods, from finely crafted shoes and belts to stylish handbags. The market's evolution mirrors Meerut's own journey—from a colonial outpost to a city that has seamlessly blended its historical roots with contemporary commerce. Tourists and locals alike flock here, seeking durable, high-quality leather products that rival global brands while retaining the distinct touch of traditional craftsmanship.

Even as Meerut embraces modernity, its traditional bazaars coexist with sleek shopping malls, creating a fascinating juxtaposition of the old and the new. The Melange Mall in Pallavapuram and other modern retail spaces offer a different shopping experience, catering to a clientele that seeks air-conditioned comfort, international brands, and entertainment hubs. Yet, rather than replacing the age-old markets, these malls have simply added another layer to the city's commercial fabric, ensuring that Meerut's retail scene caters to both the nostalgia of tradition and the convenience of modernity.

As dusk settles over Meerut's bazaars, the energy of the day transforms rather than fades; the gold merchants of Saraffa Bazaar tally their sales, leather craftsmen in Lal Kurti prepare for another day of production, and hawkers in Sadar Bazaar pack up their stalls, their voices echoing in the alleyways. These markets have withstood the rise and fall of empires, the turbulence of history, and the ever-changing tides of commerce, thriving with an unyielding spirit. Meerut's bazaars are not merely places of trade; they are living chronicles of resilience and evolution, telling the tale of a city that has long been a crossroads of history and innovation. From the historic alleys of Sadar Bazaar to the contemporary corridors of modern malls, and from the artistry of goldsmiths to the mastery of sports equipment makers, these vibrant markets stand as a testament to Meerut's glorious past while promising a dynamic, ever-evolving future.

CHAPTER EIGHTEEN

GASTRONOMIC GEMS: EXPLORING THE FOOD CULTURE OF MEERUT

It would be impossible to discuss Meerut without highlighting its culinary treasures. The culinary landscape of Meerut is a vibrant tapestry woven with flavors that tantalize the taste buds and evoke a sense of nostalgia for those who have experienced its gastronomic delights. At the heart of this culinary adventure lies the iconic Delhi Chole Bhatura, a dish that has found a special place in the hearts and stomachs of Meerut's residents. The aromatic blend of spices in the chole, simmered to perfection, paired with the pillowy soft yet crisp bhatura, creates a symphony of textures and tastes that has become synonymous with comfort food in the city.

As one meanders through the bustling streets of Meerut, the air is filled with the intoxicating aroma of Chhavni Chaat Bazaar's legendary offerings. The golgappas, crisp hollow spheres filled with a tangy tamarind water and spiced potato mixture, offer an explosion of flavors with each bite. Equally renowned is the aloo tikki chaat, where crispy potato patties are smothered in a medley of chutneys, yogurt, and crunchy sev, creating a harmonious balance of spicy, sweet, and tangy notes that dance on the palate.

No culinary journey through Meerut would be complete without a stop at A-One Ice Cream, an institution that has been delighting dessert enthusiasts for generations. Their signature vanilla ice cream, served in a glass bowl and generously topped with shredded cashews and juicy pineapple chunks, is a testament to the simple pleasures of life. The creamy sweetness of the ice cream, combined with the crunch of cashews and the tropical burst of pineapple, creates a dessert experience that lingers in memory long after the last spoonful has been savored.

As evening descends upon the city, the aroma of sizzling seekh kebabs wafts through the air, drawing food lovers to the numerous kebab stalls that dot the landscape. These succulent skewers of minced meat, infused with a blend of aromatic spices and grilled to perfection over open flames, offer a carnivorous delight that has become an integral part of Meerut's culinary identity. The smoky char on the exterior gives way to a juicy, flavorful interior that melts in the mouth, leaving diners craving for more.

For those with a sweet tooth, Meerut's traditional confections of revdi and gazzak provide a delightful indulgence. These age-old sweets, crafted from sesame seeds and jaggery, offer a satisfying crunch and a subtle sweetness that is both comforting and addictive. Often enjoyed during the winter months, these treats have become an inseparable part of Meerut's cultural fabric, passed down through generations as a symbol of warmth and celebration.

The humble yet beloved matar kulcha stands as a testament to the city's ability to elevate simple ingredients into a culinary masterpiece. Soft, leavened bread served alongside a spicy green pea curry creates a meal that is both satisfying and economical, beloved by students and workers alike as a quick and delicious lunch option. The interplay of textures between the fluffy kulcha and the creamy matar curry showcases the ingenuity of Meerut's street food culture.

As the scorching summer sun beats down upon the city, relief comes in the form of ganne ka ras, or freshly pressed sugarcane juice. This sweet elixir, extracted from the fibrous stalks of sugarcane, offers a natural and refreshing respite from the heat. Served ice-cold, often with a squeeze of lime and a pinch of salt, ganne ka ras has become an integral part of Meerut's summer rituals, with long queues forming at juice stalls across the city.

The culinary tapestry of Meerut is rich and diverse, reflecting the city's history, cultural influences, and the innovative spirit of its people. From the hearty chole bhatura to the delicate flavors of A-One's ice cream, from the spicy kick of seekh kebabs to the sweet crunch of revdi and gazzak, Meerut's food scene offers a gastronomic journey that captivates the senses and nourishes the soul. It is through these beloved dishes that the city's identity is preserved and celebrated, creating a culinary legacy that continues to evolve while honoring its roots.

QAWWALI GENEALOGY: THE SABRI LEGACY

In the vibrant tapestry of Meerut's musical heritage, the Sabri legacy stands as a testament to the enduring power of qawwali, a devotional form of music that has captivated hearts for centuries. The story of the Sabri Brothers, Ghulam Farid Sabri and Maqbool Ahmed Sabri, is not merely a tale of musical prowess but a journey that traces its roots to the courts of Mughal emperors and the mystical traditions of Sufism.

The Sabri lineage, claiming direct descent from the legendary Mian Tansen, court musician to Akbar the Great, carries with it a wealth of musical knowledge passed down through generations. This rich heritage is evident in the 19th-century raga improvisation notebooks, meticulously preserved by the family. These yellowed pages, filled with intricate notations and marginalia, offer a rare glimpse into the evolution of qawwali as an art form. The notebooks reveal a complex system of melodic elaboration, with detailed instructions on how to expand upon the skeletal structure of a raga, allowing for the spontaneous yet structured improvisations that are the hallmark of qawwali performance.

Born in 1930 in Kalyana, a village in the district of Rohtak, Punjab, Ghulam Farid Sabri began his musical journey at the tender age of six under the tutelage of his father, Inayat Hussain Sabri. The family's migration to Pakistan following the partition in 1947 marked a turning point in their musical odyssey. Amidst the hardships of refugee life in Karachi, Ghulam Farid's dedication to his art remained unwavering. His nightly vigils of zikr, lasting four to five hours for two years, not only strengthened his lungs but also forged the magnificent voice that would later enthrall millions.

The Sabri Brothers' rise to prominence in the 1970s and 1980s coincided with significant technological advancements in sound reproduction. Their adaptation to sound system technology marked a pivotal moment in qawwali's evolution. The introduction of electric harmoniums and sophisticated microphone techniques allowed for a more nuanced capture of the qawwals' vocal intricacies. This technological embrace enabled the Sabri Brothers to fill vast concert halls and outdoor venues without sacrificing the intimacy and spiritual fervor of their performances.

The Sabri legacy, however, extends far beyond their groundbreaking use of technology. Their repertoire, a blend of traditional Sufi poetry and original compositions, showcased their mastery of multiple languages including Urdu, Persian, and Punjabi. Ghulam Farid Sabri's own poetic contributions, such as "Aawe Mahi" and "Auliyao'n Ke Maula Imam Aaye Hai," added new dimensions to the qawwali canon, demonstrating the genre's capacity for innovation within its classical framework.

In recent years, the Sabri tradition has found new expression through youth fusion experiments with electronic dance music (EDM). This contemporary interpretation of qawwali, while controversial among purists, has introduced the genre to a new generation of listeners. Young musicians, inspired by the Sabri Brothers' legacy, have begun incorporating electronic beats and synthesizers into traditional qawwali structures, creating a unique sound that bridges centuries of musical tradition with modern sensibilities.

The Sabri Brothers' influence on qawwali extends beyond their musical innovations. Their performances, characterized by a gradual build in tempo and energy, exemplify the art of inducing a state of spiritual ecstasy known as "sama." This transcendent experience, central to the Sufi tradition, is achieved through a careful orchestration of melodic improvisation, rhythmic intensity, and lyrical depth.

As we delve into the Sabri legacy, we uncover a musical lineage that has not only preserved the essence of qawwali but has also continually reinvented it. From the handwritten notations in century-old notebooks to the pulsing beats of EDM-infused performances, the Sabri tradition embodies the dynamic nature of this devotional art form. In Meerut and beyond, the echoes of Ghulam Farid and Maqbool Ahmed Sabri's voices continue to resonate, inspiring new generations to explore the spiritual and musical depths of qawwali.

CHAPTER TWENTY

NAUCHANDI MELA: THE HEARTBEAT OF MEERUT'S FESTIVE SPIRIT

As the second Sunday after Holi approaches each year, the sleepy Nauchandi Ground in Meerut undergoes a remarkable metamorphosis, transforming into a vibrant, pulsating ephemeral city that sprawls across five square kilometers. The Nauchandi Mela, a month-long extravaganza that traces its roots back to the late 1600s, stands as a testament to the enduring power of temporary urbanism and the human capacity for creating order amidst seeming chaos.

This annual fair, organized alternately by the Municipal Corporation of Meerut and the Zila Panchayat, draws an astonishing 50,000 visitors daily, necessitating an intricate web of temporary infrastructure that rivals many permanent urban settlements. Pathways wind through the fairground, lined with hundreds of stalls offering a kaleidoscope of goods from across India. The air is thick with the aroma of sizzling street food, the cacophony of hawkers' calls, and the excited chatter of fairgoers.

The governance of this transient metropolis presents a fascinating study in crowd-sourced models of urban management. While the official organizers provide the broad framework, it is the collective will and unspoken rules of the thousands of visitors and vendors that truly shape the fair's day-to-day operations. Informal committees of stallholders emerge to resolve disputes, manage waste, and ensure the smooth flow of foot traffic. This organic, bottom-up approach to governance stands in stark contrast to the top-down planning of permanent cities, offering valuable insights into alternative models of urban organization.

At the heart of the Nauchandi Mela lies a rich tradition of transmedia storytelling that has evolved over centuries. The fair serves as a living repository of oral histories, folk performances, and cultural narratives that are passed down and transformed with each iteration. The once-popular cinema shows and nautankis (traditional theater) may have waned in recent years, but they have given way to new forms of storytelling. Today, social media influencers mingle with traditional bards, creating a unique blend of ancient and modern narrative techniques that keep the fair's stories alive and relevant for new generations.

The Nauchandi Mela is more than just a fair; it is a powerful symbol of communal harmony in a region that has seen its share of religious tensions. The fairground is home to both the Chandi Devi temple and the dargah of Bale Miyan, standing as silent sentinels to the fair's inclusive spirit. This coexistence of Hindu and Muslim shrines, both welcoming devotees of all faiths, embodies the syncretic culture that the fair has nurtured over centuries.

As the sun sets each evening during the fair's run, the Nauchandi Ground transforms once again. The daytime bustle gives way to a nocturnal wonderland of twinkling lights, thrilling rides, and mesmerizing performances. Giant wheels and death-defying stunts draw crowds well into the night, while the aroma of Meerut's famous halwa paratha wafts through the air, tempting visitors to indulge in one last treat before heading home.

Yet, for all its timeless charm, the Nauchandi Mela faces modern challenges. Recent years have seen a decline in attendance, attributed to changing entertainment preferences and urban development pressures. The fair's organizers grapple with the delicate balance of preserving traditions while innovating to attract new audiences. Proposals for introducing hot-air balloon rides and improving visitor accommodations signal a recognition of the need to evolve while maintaining the fair's essential character.

As dawn breaks over Meerut each day during the Nauchandi Mela, this ephemeral city awakens once more, ready to weave new stories into its centuries-old tapestry. In its fleeting existence, it offers a profound reflection on the nature of urban life, community, and the enduring human desire for connection and celebration.

CHAPTER TWENTY-ONE

MEERUT'S FUTURE - A SYNTHESIS OF HERITAGE AND PROGRESS

As we conclude our exploration of Meerut's rich tapestry, we find a city poised between its illustrious past and a future full of promise and challenges. From its Harappan origins to its pivotal role in the 1857 Uprising, and its evolution into a modern industrial hub, Meerut has consistently reinvented itself while maintaining its core identity.

The path forward for Meerut lies in its ability to leverage its unique strengths while addressing pressing issues. The city's renowned sports goods sector, which produces an impressive 70% of India's sports equipment, stands on the brink of a technological revolution. Embracing cutting-edge technologies and sustainable practices will be vital for maintaining its global competitiveness. Meanwhile, the ambitious Ganga-Jamuna Smart Ecotone Project offers a bold vision for sustainable urban development, presenting an opportunity to redefine the relationship between the city and its rivers, ultimately creating a harmonious balance between urban growth and ecological preservation.

Education will play a pivotal role in shaping Meerut's future trajectory. With 17 engineering colleges producing thousands of graduates annually, the city must bridge the yawning gap between academic knowledge and practical skills. Initiatives like proposed IT parks and incubation centers could nurture entrepreneurship and innovation among the youth, ensuring they are equipped to thrive in an increasingly competitive world.

The ongoing transformation of Meerut's transportation infrastructure, particularly with the Delhi-Meerut Rapid Rail Transit System, opens new vistas for economic growth and regional integration. This new corridor will significantly reduce travel time between Delhi and Meerut, reshaping the economic landscape. As Meerut becomes more closely integrated with the National Capital Region, it must carefully manage this relationship to preserve its unique cultural identity while capitalizing on increased economic opportunities.

Perhaps one of the greatest challenges—and opportunities—facing Meerut lies in fostering social harmony and inclusive growth. The city's diverse neighborhoods must learn to celebrate their differences while striving toward common goals. Incidents like the protests against Muslim families moving into Hindu-majority areas highlight the need for concerted efforts to promote understanding and cooperation across religious and social divides. Yet, events such as the Nauchandi

Mela—a 350-year-old tradition that draws people from all communities—offer a glimpse of what is possible when various groups come together in celebration.

As we peer into the future, it is evident that Meerut's success will hinge on striking a delicate balance between tradition and innovation, local identity and global aspirations, as well as economic growth and environmental sustainability. The city's rich history is preserved in its landmarks like the Basilica of Our Lady of Graces in Sardhana and the Augarnath Temple, as well as in its archives and collective memories.

In conclusion, Meerut stands at a critical juncture, poised between its storied past and a future brimming with potential. By drawing upon the wisdom encapsulated in its heritage, the skills and resilience of its people, and the vision of its leaders, Meerut has the opportunity to pen a new chapter in its long history—one that could see it emerge as a paragon of sustainable, inclusive urban development for cities across India and beyond. As it marches forward, Meerut carries with it the hopes, dreams, and narratives of countless generations, each contributing to the ongoing saga of this remarkable place. The Meerut of tomorrow, while rooted in its rich past, has the potential to be a beacon of progress, harmony, and innovation in the heart of India.

References

1. Britannica, T. Editors of encyclopedia (n.d.). *Ganges-Yamuna Doab*. Encyclopedia Britannica. Retrieved from https://www.britannica.com/place/Ganges-Yamuna-Doab

2. Singh, I. B. (n.d.). *GEOLOGICAL EVOLUTION OF GANGA PLAIN : AN OVERVIEW*. Semantic Scholar. Retrieved from https://www.semanticscholar.org/paper/GEOLOGICAL-EVOLUTION-OF-GANGA-PLAIN-:-AN-OVERVIEW-Singh/3ee160eb5b3af59d906b5bd432ecd7bc22ac06f7

3. Joshi, V. B. (2022). *Ganga Plain: A Cradle of Human Civilization*. NCAS Journal, *12*(2).

4. Sinha, R., & Tandon, S. K. (2024). Coupled role of climate and tectonics in the evolution of the fluvial systems of the Indo-Gangetic Plains, India. *Journal of Sedimentary Research*, 94(5), 559–579.

5. National Mission for Clean Ganga. (2019). *India Water Week 2019 Presentation 4.*

6. Next IAS. (n.d.). *Indo-Gangetic Plains*. https://www.nextias.com/blog/indo-gangetic-plains/

7. SCIRP. (n.d.). *Study on the Evolution of the Yamuna River and its Relationship with the Development of the Harappan Civilization.* https://www.scirp.org/journal/paperinformation?paperid=114380

8. National Institutes of Health. (n.d.). *Retrieved from the National Institutes of Health website.* https://www.ncbi.nlm.nih.gov/articles/PMC6979522/

9. Kumar, A., & Rai, S. C. (2016). Indo-Gangetic Plains: Evolution and Later Developments. *Aquatic Procedia, 4,*

1050–1057. https://doi.org/ https://www.researchgate.net/publication/ 300216107_Indo-Gangetic_Plains_Evolution_and_Later_Developments

10. National Mission for Clean Ganga & NEERI. (n.d.). *Ganga Report.* https://nmcg.nic.in/writereaddata/ fileupload/NMCGNEERI%20Ganga%20Report.pdf

11. ResearchGate. (n.d.). *Map of the Gangetic plain showing different tectonic features.* Retrieved from https://www.researchgate.net/figure/Map-of-the-Gangetic-plain-showing-different-tectonic-features-1-Solani-fault-2_fig1_223624492

12. Sinha, R., & Tandon, S. K. (2024). Coupled role of climate and tectonics in the evolution of the fluvial systems of the Indo-Gangetic Plains, India. *Journal of Sedimentary Research, 94*(5), 559–579. https://doi.org/ https://pubs.geoscienceworld.org/sepm/jsedres/ article/94/5/559/648515/Coupled-role-of-climate-and-tectonics-in-the

13. Palaeontological Society of India. (n.d.). *Journal of the Palaeontological Society of India.* http://www.palaeontologicalsociety.in/vol41/v13.pdf

14. Geological Society of India. (n.d.). *Journal of the Geological Society of India.* https://www.geosocindia.org/index.php/jgsi/article/ view/173848?articlesBySimilarityPage=41

15. ResearchGate. (n.d.). *Maps of Ganga Basin and Ganga-Yamuna Doab.* Retrieved from https://www.researchgate.net/figure/Maps-of-Ganga-Basin-and-Ganga-Yamuna-Doab-Prayagraj-India-a-DEM-map-of-Ganga-Basin_fig1_356727763

16. Columbia University Press. (n.d.). *The Ganges.* https://doi.org/https://colab.ws/articles/

10.2307%2F621126

17. Ghosal, K., & others. (2022). Spatiotemporal Evolution of the Yamuna River System Since the Last Glacial Maximum. *Geophysical Research Letters*, 49(1). https://doi.org/ https://agupubs.onlinelibrary.wiley.com/doi/full/ 10.1029/2021GL096100

18. Geological Society of India. (n.d.). *Journal of the Geological Society of India.* https://www.geosocindia.org/index.php/jgsi/article/ view/173297?articlesBySimilarityPage=32

19. PMF IAS. (n.d.). *Ganga-Brahmaputra River System.* https://www.pmfias.com/ganga-brahmaputra-river- system-tributaries-ganga-yamuna-brahmaputra/

20. DNTB. (n.d.). *Hydrology.* https://ouci.dntb.gov.ua/en/ works/4KeevON9/

21. Jain, M., & others. (2023). Geochemical evidence for west-flowing paleo-Yamuna River in northwest India during the late Quaternary and its implication for the Harappan Civilization. *Journal of Asian Earth Sciences*, 252, 110688.

22. WorldAtlas. (n.d.). *What is a Doab?.* https://www.worldatlas.com/articles/what-is-a- doab.html

23. Geological Society of India. (n.d.). *Journal of the Geological Society of India.* https://www.geosocindia.org/index.php/jgsi/article/ view/173297?articlesBySimilarityPage=25

24. Eureka Alert. (n.d.). *New study reveals how the Indus Civilization's decline was linked to a shift in monsoon patterns.* https://eurekamag.com/research/001/076/ 001076214.php

25. Times of India. (2021, July 26). *70 yrs on, Hastinapur*

excavations looking for Mahabharata link. https://timesofindia.indiatimes.com/city/meerut/70-yrs-on-hastinapur-excavations-looking-for-mahabharata-link/articleshow/84563388.cms

26. Jatland. (n.d.). *Kurukshetra War.* https://www.jatland.com/home/Kurukshetra_War

27. HinduPost. (n.d.). *Hastinapur excavation gives insight of Bharat.* https://hindupost.in/history/hastinapur-excavation-gives-insight-of-bharat/

28. Economic Times. (2019, October 20). *Mahabharata much older, say ASI archaeologists.* https://economictimes.com/news/politics-and-nation/mahabharata-much-older-say-asi-archaeologists/articleshow/71658119.cms

29. Pragyata. (n.d.). *The cut-off date in the Mahabharata debate.* https://pragyata.com/the-cut-off-date-in-the-mahabharata-debate/

30. News18. (n.d.). *Dating the Mahabharata to 2000 BC: Archaeologists shift from Painted Grey Ware to Ochre Coloured Pottery.* https://www.news18.com/news/india/dating-the-mahabharata-to-2000-bc-archaeologists-shift-from-painted-grey-ware-to-ochre-coloured-pottery-1864423.html

31. Durgesh, P. (n.d.). *Hastinapur.* Lucknow University. https://www.lkouniv.ac.in/site/writereaddata/siteContent/202003281454237573durgesh_Hastinapur.pdf

32. Rao, K. M. (2009, August 2). *The Mahabharata War: The veracity of epic proved by recent archaeological excavations.* https://kmrao.wordpress.com/2009/08/02/the-mahabharata-war-the-veracity-of-epic-proved-by-recent-archaeological-excavations/

33. Goodreads. (n.d.). *Historicity of the Mahabharata.*

Retrieved from https://www.goodreads.com/book/show/36291745-historicity-of-the-mahabharata

34. Jyotish Bhawan India. (n.d.). *Mahabharata – An Archaeological Look to Historical Facts.* https://jyotishbhawanindia.com/mahabharata-an-archaeological-look-to-historical-facts/

35. IJRASET. (n.d.). *Ancients Ruins of Mahabharata Prominence Hastinapur.* https://www.ijraset.com/research-paper/ancients-ruins-of-mahabharata-prominence-hastinapur

36. Economic Times. (2019, October 20). *Mahabharata much older, say ASI archaeologists.* https://economictimes.com/news/politics-and-nation/mahabharata-much-older-say-asi-archaeologists/articleshow/71658119.cms

37. Wikipedia contributors. (2024, May 17). *Hastinapur.* Wikipedia. Retrieved from https://en.wikipedia.org/wiki/Hastinapur

38. BooksFact. (n.d.). *Archaeological excavations prove veracity Mahabharata war around 3100 BCE.* https://www.booksfact.com/archeology/archaeological-excavations-prove-veracity-mahabharata-war-around-3100-bce.html

39. Kumar, A., & Rai, S. C. (2022). Ancients Ruins of Mahabharata Prominence Hastinapur Giving Vindication of Bioarchaeology. *International Journal of Multidisciplinary Research and Modern Education, 14*(1), 108–112.

40. Safvi, R. (n.d.). *Vidur ka Tila and Archaeological Mound in Hastinapur.* https://ranasafvi.com/vidur-ka-tila-and-archaeological-mound-in-hastinapur/

41. Holidify. (n.d.). *Vidur ka Tila, Meerut.* https://www.holidify.com/places/meerut/-vidur-ka-

tila-sightseeing-1254420.html

42. Times of India. (n.d.). *Mahabharata: Battle, myth or reality?*. https://timesofindia.indiatimes.com/life-style/soul-search/mahabharata-battle-myth-or-reality/photostory/106129018.cms

43. Times of India. (2021, July 26). *70 yrs on, Hastinapur excavations looking for Mahabharata link.* https://timesofindia.indiatimes.com/city/meerut/70-yrs-on-hastinapur-excavations-looking-for-mahabharata-link/articleshow/84563388.cms

44. Varnam. (2013, May 5). *Mahabharata date based on archaeology.* https://www.varnam.org/2013/05/05/mahabharata-date-based-on-archaeology/

45. The Social Digest. (2024, March 4). *Mysteries of Mahabharata: Exploring archaeological evidence and historical context.* https://thesocialdigest.com/2024/03/04/mysteries-of-mahabharata-exploring-archaeological-evidence-and-historical-context/

46. Civilsdaily. (n.d.). *Significance of Meerut.* https://www.civilsdaily.com/news/significance-of-meerut/

47. Scroll.in. (2017, August 29). *Interview: 'Can the Mahabharata actually be treated as literal history?'.* https://scroll.in/article/857249/interview-can-the-mahabharata-actually-be-treated-as-literal-history

48. ThePrint. (2023, June 29). *How the 2008 Alamgirpur re-excavation challenged timeline of 'mighty' Harappan civilisation.* https://theprint.in/opinion/how-the-2008-alamgirpur-re-excavation-challenged-timeline-of-mighty-harappan-civilisation/1745312/

49. HD Heritage Walks. (2023, August 28). *Alamgirpur Archaeological Site (aka Parshuram ka Tila, Khera Alamgirpur, Meerut District, Uttar Pradesh).*

https://hdheritagewalks.wordpress.com/2023/08/28/alamgirpur-archaeological-site-aka-parshuram-ka-tila-khera-alamgirpur-meerut-district-uttar-pradesh/

50. Our Ancient World. (n.d.). *Alamgirpur*. http://ourancientworld.com/Settlement.aspx?id=361

51. iLearnCANA. (n.d.). *Alamgirpur*. https://ilearncana.com/details/Alamgirpur/1581

52. Vivekanand International Foundation. (n.d.). *Alamgirpur Excavations*. Academia.edu.

53. Business Standard. (2016, June 27). *Harappans in Alamgirpur made clever use of landscape, water availability*. https://www.business-standard.com/article/news-ians/harappans-in-alamgirpur-made-clever-use-of-landscape-water-availability-116062701057_1.html

54. Sacred Footsteps. (2022, September 5). *The Sufis of Kochi, South India*. https://sacredfootsteps.com/2022/09/05/the-sufis-of-kochi-south-india/

55. Haji Ali Dargah Trust. (n.d.). *History of Haji Ali Dargah*. https://www.hajialidargah.in/hajiali_history1.html

56. IslamOnWeb. (n.d.). *Hadith: A Persistent Tradition in Indian Culture*. https://en.islamonweb.net/hadith-a-persistent-tradition-in-indian-culture

57. Kashmir Reader. (2024, October 14). *Saints' story: Rafiabad's legendary mystic, the enduring legacy of Hazrat Syed Malik Bukhari (RA)*. https://kashmirreader.com/2024/10/14/saints-story-rafiabads-legendary-mystic-the-enduring-legacy-of-hazrat-syed-malik-bukhari-ra/

58. Muslim Central. (n.d.). *Ismail Kamdar: Imam Al-Bukhari – Life, Works, Legacy*. https://muslimcentral.com/ismail-kamdar-imam-al-bukhari-life-works-legacy/

59. Rishihoood University. (2022). *Urban Development in 18th Century*. https://journal.rishihood.edu.in/wp-

content/uploads/2022/02/
5-Urban_Development_in_18th_Century-1.pdf

60. UNESCO World Heritage Centre. (n.d.). *Maratha Military Architecture in Maharashtra.* https://whc.unesco.org/en/tentativelists/6533/

61. PMF IAS. (n.d.). *Maratha Military Landscapes.* https://www.pmfias.com/maratha-military-landscapes/

62. Srivastava, A. (n.d.). *Maratha Military Landscapes, India.* LinkedIn. Retrieved from https://www.linkedin.com/pulse/maratha-military-landscapes-india-ayush-srivastava-ivkhc

63. Times of India. (2023, July 26). *Historic Maratha war memorial in Pune faces neglect amid rising urbanization.* https://timesofindia.indiatimes.com/city/pune/historic-maratha-war-memorial-in-pune-faces-neglect-amid-rising-urbanization/articleshow/115125223.cms

64. GACBE. (n.d.). *[Material on Urban Planning - Title not readily available].* https://gacbe.ac.in/pdf/ematerial/18BDS33C-U1.pdf *(Note: This link goes to a PDF with a course code but no clear title.)*

65. Joshi, P. (n.d.). *1857, or Can the Indian Mutiny Be Fixed?.* Branch Collective. https://branchcollective.org/?ps_articles=priti-joshi-1857-or-can-the-indian-mutiny-be-fixed

66. Bayly, C. A. (2010). Empire and Locality: A Global Dimension to the 1857 Indian Uprising. *Journal of Global History*, 5(1), 27–54. https://www.cambridge.org/core/journals/journal-of-global-history/article/empire-and-locality-a-global-dimension-to-the-1857-indian-uprising/95B04AF03938B634F3A0D51D72AFDB02

67. Britannica, T. Editors of encyclopedia (n.d.). *Indian*

Rebellion of 1857. Encyclopedia Britannica. Retrieved from https://www.britannica.com/event/Indian-Rebellion-of-1857

68. Khan, I. (2017). *The role of rumour in the Indian Rebellion of 1857.* (University of Glasgow thesis). https://theses.gla.ac.uk/71385/1/10390997.pdf

69. PW Only IAS. (n.d.). *1857 Revolt: Communication & Leadership – Detailed Exploration.* https://pwonlyias.com/ncert-notes/1857-revolt-communication-leadership-detailed-exploration/

70. Asian Development Bank. (n.d.). *[Project Document - Title Not Readily Available].* https://www.adb.org/sites/default/files/project-documents/51073/51073-002-rp-en_1.pdf*(Note: This ADB document needs a proper title for citation.)*

71. Meerut Development Authority. (n.d.). *History of Meerut.* https://mdameerut.in/history.php

72. Singh, C. (1982). *Who Is A Casteist – An Analysis.*

73. Economic Times. (2016, December 1). *More than 8000 acres of vacant rail land to grow farm products.* https://economictimes.com/industry/transportation/railways/more-than-8000-acres-of-vacant-rail-land-to-grow-farm-products/articleshow/56122575.cms

74. Census of India. (1931). *Census of India, 1931, Volume I - India, Part I - Report.* http://piketty.pse.ens.fr/files/ideologie/data/CensusIndia/CensusIndia1931/CensusIndia1931IndiaReport.pdf

75. Macrotrends. (n.d.). *Meerut Population 2024.* https://www.macrotrends.net/cities/21332/meerut/population

76. Meerut District Administration. (n.d.). *Demography.* https://meerut.nic.in/demography/

77. Regional Centre for Urban and Environmental Studies,

Lucknow. (n.d.). *Compendium of Urban Data (Uttar Pradesh): Population Growth of ULB in UP 1901-2001.*

78. Census of India. (1951). *District Census Handbook: Meerut.* https://censusindia.gov.in/nada/index.php/catalog/28734/download/31916/20829_1951_MEE.pdf

79. Meerut GDP. (n.d.). *Current Sectoral Status of Economy of Meerut: Sports Goods.* https://meerutgdp.com/current-sectoral-status-of-economy-of-meerut/sports-goods

80. Invest UP. (2023, June). *Comprehensive Action Plan for Sustainable Development of Meerut Region.* https://invest.up.gov.in/wp-content/uploads/2023/06/can-smart_060623.pdf

81. Times of India. (2023, August 1). *Path ahead for Meerut's sports goods industry.* https://timesofindia.indiatimes.com/city/meerut/path-ahead-for-meeruts-sports-goods-industry/articleshow/115881861.cms

82. Times of India. (2014, August 28). *Bat like Meerut.* https://timesofindia.indiatimes.com/city/meerut/bat-like-meerut/articleshow/40067844.cms

83. ITLN. (n.d.). *Allcargo Gati expands reach in Meerut sports cluster, rebrands AFVs.* https://www.itln.in/logistics/allcargo-gati-expands-reach-in-meerut-sports-cluster-rebrands-afvs-1353520

84. Sharma, A. (n.d.). *Chapter 4: Sports Goods Industry in Meerut.* Academia.edu. https://www.academia.edu/28449829/Chapter_4_Sports_Goods_Industry_in_Meerut

85. Swarajya. (n.d.). *Meerut Metro trial begins to connect with RRTS network at key station, reducing traffic congestion on roads to Delhi.* https://swarajyamag.com/news-brief/

meerut-metro-trial-begins-to-connect-with-rrts-network-at-key-station-reducing-traffic-congestion-on-roads-to-delhi

86. Higher Education Digest. (n.d.). *Meerut Institute of Engineering and Technology.* https://www.highereducationdigest.com/meerut-institute-of-engineering-and-technology/

87. National Capital Region Planning Board. (n.d.). *Chapter 2: Comprehensive Mobility Plan for NCR.* https://ncrpb.nic.in/pdf_files/05_chapter%202_cma.pdf

88. Meerut GDP. (n.d.). *Executive Summary.* https://meerutgdp.com/executive-summary

89. National Capital Region Planning Board. (n.d.). *Functional Plan on ground for NCR.* https://ncrpb.nic.in/pdf_files/FunctionalPlanongroundforNCR.pdf

90. Meerut Development Authority. (n.d.). *Acts & Description.* https://mdameerut.in/act_desc.php

91. UPGRO. (n.d.). *Roads for Water.* https://upgro.org/catalyst-projects/roads-for-water/

92. Centre for Water and Sanitation. (n.d.). *Rainwater Harvesting Guidelines.* https://cwas.org.in/resources/file_manager/module_3-3_1_rwh_guidelines.pdf

93. International Journal of Technology and Human Consciousness. (2024). *[Article Title Not Available].* *International Journal of Technology and Human Consciousness.* https://journals.stmjournals.com/ijthc/article=2024/view=183963/ *(Note: This link leads to a journal page; the specific article title is required.)*

94. KrakenSense. (n.d.). *The Impacts of Urbanization on Aquifer Recharge.* https://krakensense.com/blog/the-impacts-of-urbanization-on-aquifer-recharge

95. Uttar Pradesh Expressways Industrial Development

Authority. (2021). *UPEIDA Land Development & Building Regulations 2021.*

96. MeerutWants. (n.d.). *Know about Nauchandi Mela, the famous annual fair of Meerut.* https://www.meerutwants.com/new-on-meerutwants/know-about-nauchandi-mela-the-famous-annual-fair-of-meerut

97. Times of India. (2016, April 20). *10 days after inauguration, iconic Nauchandi fair awaits stalls, visitors.* https://timesofindia.indiatimes.com/city/meerut/10-days-after-inauguration-iconic-nauchandi-fair-awaits-stalls-visitors/articleshow/58035114.cms

98. Homegrown. (n.d.). *How an annual mela in Meerut became a symbol of Hindu-Muslim unity.* https://homegrown.co.in/homegrown-explore/how-an-annual-mela-in-meerut-became-a-symbol-of-hindu-muslim-unity

99. Economic Times. (2011, March 1). *Nauchandi mela in Meerut loses bling on lack of crowd pull factor.* [https://economictimes.com/north/nauchandi-mela-in-meerut-loses-bling-on-lack-of-crowd-pull-factor/articleshow/1274

100. Asia Society. (n.d.). *Qawwali: The Art of Devotional Singing.* https://asiasociety.org/qawwali-and-art-devotional-singing

101. Riyaaz Qawwali. (n.d.). *Sabri Brothers.* https://riyaazqawwali.com/sabri-brothers/

102. Serenade Magazine. (n.d.). *Qawwali Music: Unveiling the Soulful Sounds and Spiritual Poetry of India.* https://serenademagazine.com/qawwali-music-unveiling-the-soulful-sounds-and-spiritual-poetry-of-india/

103. Maqbool Sabri (WordPress Blog). (n.d.). *Sabri Brothers.*

https://maqboolsabri.wordpress.com/sabri-brothers/

104. The News Minute. (2016, June 23). *Tribute: Amjad Sabri, inheritor of a rich Sufi legacy.* https://www.thenewsminute.com/features/tribute-amjad-sabri-inheritor-rich-sufi-legacy-45427

105. USI of India. (n.d.). *Meerut Cantonment and the War of Independence 1857.* https://www.usiofindia.org/publication-journal/meerut-cantonment-and-the-war-of-independence-1857.html

106. Meerut Development Authority. (n.d.). *History of Meerut.* https://mdameerut.in/history.php

107. Economic Times. (2012, June 18). *Meerut's Bombay Bazaar furniture market enjoys a loyal clientele from entire western UP and NCR.* https://economictimes.com/north/meeruts-bombay-bazaar-furniture-market-enjoys-a-loyal-clientele-from-entire-western-up-and-ncr/articleshow/15446368.cms

108. Meerut District Administration. (n.d.). *Culture & Heritage.* https://meerut.nic.in/culture-heritage/

109. Indianetzone. (n.d.). *Meerut.* https://www.indianetzone.com/meerut

110. Scroll.in. (2017, March 29). *How can we share our neighbourhood with a Muslim? In Meerut, now there's talk of 'land jihad'.* https://scroll.in/article/862216/how-can-we-share-our-neighbourhood-with-a-muslim-in-meerut-now-theres-talk-of-land-jihad

111. Meerut District Administration. (n.d.). *History.* https://meerut.nic.in/history/

112. Britannica, T. Editors of encyclopedia (n.d.). *Meerut.* Encyclopedia Britannica. Retrieved from https://www.britannica.com/place/Meerut

113. Catholic Shrine Basilica. (n.d.). *Basilica of Our Lady of Graces, Sardhana.* https://catholicshrinebasilica.com/

basilica-of-our-lady-of-graces-sardhana/

114. Outlook Traveller. (n.d.). *The tale of a Meerut church built by a begum who commanded an army.* https://www.outlooktraveller.com/experiences/heritage/the-tale-of-a-meerut-church-built-by-a-begum-who-commanded-an-army

115. Delhi Archives. (n.d.). *Oral History Programme.* https://delhiarchives.delhi.gov.in/archives/oral-history-programme

116. Local Welcome. (n.d.). *Oral Histories.* https://www.localwelcome.org/oral-histories

117. Uttar Pradesh State Archives. (n.d.). *History of Archives in Uttar Pradesh.* https://uparchives.up.nic.in/history.html

118. International Journal of Engineering Research & Technology. (n.d.). *Urban Area Mapping of Meerut City and its Environs Using Quickbird Satellite Data and Geographical Information System (GIS) Techniques. International Journal of Engineering Research & Technology,* 4(12). https://www.ijert.org/research/urban-area-mapping-of-meerut-city-and-its-environs-using-quickbird-satellite-data-and-geographical-information-system-gis-techniques-IJERTV4IS020120.pdf

119. Tornos India. (n.d.). *Indian Mutiny Event Dateline.* https://tornosindia.com/indian-mutiny-event-dateline/

120. National Atlas & Thematic Mapping Organisation. (n.d.). *Meerut.* https://geoportal.natmo.gov.in/dataset/meerut

121. Maps of India. (n.d.). *1857 Revolt Map.* https://www.mapsofindia.com/maps/india/rebellion-of-1857.html

122. TravelSetu. (n.d.). *Bhole Ki Jhaal Tourism.* https://travelsetu.com/guide/bhole-ki-jhaal-tourism/bhole-ki-jhaal-tourism-history

123. Monstropedia. (n.d.). *Mayasura.* https://www.monstropedia.org/index.php?title=Mayasura

124. MeerutBN. (n.d.). *Meerut History.* https://meerutbn.com/meerut-history/

125. Meerut District Administration. (n.d.). *History.* https://meerut.nic.in/history/

126. Meerut Online. (n.d.). *Major Historic Events of Meerut.* https://www.meerutonline.in/guide/major-historic-events-of-meerut

127. IndiaStatDistricts. (n.d.). *Meerut District, Uttar Pradesh.* https://www.indiastatdistricts.com/uttarpradesh/meerut-district

128. Meerut Online. (n.d.). *About Meerut.* https://www.meerutonline.in/guide/about-meerut

129. Living to Tell a Tale (WordPress Blog). (2017, September 2). *Meerut's Nauchandi Mela: A confluence of different faiths.* https://livingtotellatale.wordpress.com/2017/09/02/meeruts-nauchandi-mela-a-confluence-of-different-faiths/

130. Times of India. (2019, April 16). *Nauchandi: Sufi saint behind 1,000-year fair.* https://timesofindia.indiatimes.com/city/meerut/nauchandi-sufi-saint-behind-1000-year-fair/articleshow/69135501.cms

131. Homegrown. (n.d.). *How an annual mela in Meerut became a symbol of Hindu-Muslim unity.* https://homegrown.co.in/homegrown-explore/how-an-annual-mela-in-meerut-became-a-symbol-of-hindu-muslim-unity

132. Saanvi Modi (WordPress Blog). (2019, August 23). *Nauchandi Mela: Discovering Meerut's iconic annual fair.* https://saanvimodi.wordpress.com/2019/08/23/nauchandi-mela-discovering-meeruts-iconic-annual-fair/

133. MeerutWants. (n.d.). *Know about Nauchandi Mela, the famous annual fair of Meerut.* https://www.meerutwants.com/new-on-meerutwants/know-about-nauchandi-mela-the-famous-annual-fair-of-meerut

134. Times of India. (2018, November 11). *Netas should respect history like we respect Atalji, scion of Meerut's Mughal-era nobleman.* https://timesofindia.indiatimes.com/city/meerut/netas-should-respect-history-like-we-respect-atalji-scion-of-meeruts-mughal-era-nobleman/articleshow/66659672.cms

135. Times of India. (2015, August 28). *Make Abu ka Maqbara a protected monument, MDA tells ASI.* https://timesofindia.indiatimes.com/city/meerut/make-abu-ka-maqbara-a-protected-monument-mda-tells-asi/articleshow/48925320.cms

About The Author

Born and raised in Meerut, Uttar Pradesh, Ashish's early years were steeped in the rich cultural tapestry of one of India's oldest cities. This background instilled in him a deep appreciation for history and a keen interest in the stories that shape communities.

Through this book, he aims to bridge the gap between academic history and public interest, making the rich tapestry of Meerut's heritage accessible to a global audience while inspiring current residents to take pride in their city's remarkable journey through time.

Ashish earned his Engineering degree from the prestigious BITS Pilani, equipping him with analytical skills that shape his writing and research. His Executive MBA from SP Jain School of Global Management further broadened his worldview, enhancing his ability to analyze complex social and economic dynamics woven into Meerut's past, present, and future. A Senior Specialist at DEWA in Dubai, he works at the intersection of sustainable energy and technology.

Ashish's passion for sharing knowledge and insights led him to become a prolific writer on LinkedIn, where his articles on various aspects of management and technology, as well as cultural observations, have garnered a significant following.

When not writing or working, Ashish enjoys learning soft skills as well as technical skills through various short courses available on LinkedIn Learning.

Ashish can be reached through his following LinkedIn handle: https://www.linkedin.com/in/ashishagarwalbits/